THE ANTISOCIAL NETWORK

ALSO BY BEN MEZRICH

NONFICTION

Bitcoin Billionaires
Woolly
The 37th Parallel
Once Upon a Time in Russia
Straight Flush
Sex on the Moon
The Accidental Billionaires
Rigged
Busting Vegas
Ugly Americans
Bringing Down the House/21

STANDALONE NOVELS

Seven Wonders
The Carrier (as Holden Scott)
Skin
Skeptic (as Holden Scott)
Fertile Ground
Reaper
Threshold

MIDDLE GRADE

Charlie Numbers and the Woolly Mammoth (with Tonya
Mezrich)
Charlie Numbers and the Man in the Moon (with Tonya
Mezrich)
Bringing Down the Mouse

NOVELLAS

Q

THE
ANTISOCIAL
NETWORK

*The GameStop Short Squeeze and the
Ragtag Group of Amateur Traders That
Brought Wall Street to Its Knees*

BEN MEZRICH

GRAND CENTRAL
PUBLISHING

NEW YORK   BOSTON

Cover design by Keenan
Cover copyright © 2021 by Hachette Book Group, Inc.

Grand Central Publishing
Hachette Book Group
1290 Avenue of the Americas, New York, NY 10104
grandcentralpublishing.com
twitter.com/grandcentralpub

First edition: September 2021

Grand Central Publishing is a division of Hachette Book Group, Inc. The Grand Central Publishing name and logo is a trademark of Hachette Book Group, Inc.

The publisher is not responsible for websites (or their content) that are not owned by the publisher.

The Hachette Speakers Bureau provides a wide range of authors for speaking events. To find out more, go to www.hachettespeakersbureau.com or call (866) 376-6591.

Print book interior design by Sean Ford

Library of Congress Control Number: 2021939248

ISBNs: 978-1-5387-0755-5 (hardcover), 978-1-5387-0758-6 (ebook), 978-1-5387-0779-1 (international)

Printed in the United States of America

LSC-C

Printing 1, 2021

For Asher and Arya, who basically lived at GameStop on Boylston until the pandemic hit; and for Bugsy, who was always right there beside them.

AUTHOR'S NOTE

The Antisocial Network is a dramatic, narrative account of one of the most unique moments in Wall Street history, based on dozens of interviews, multiple first-person sources, hours of testimony, and thousands of pages of documents, including records from a number of court proceedings. Though there are different and often contentious opinions about some of the events in the story, to the best of my ability, I re-created the scenes in the book based on the information I uncovered. Some dialogue has been re-created. In some instances, certain descriptions and character names have been altered at the request of my sources to protect privacy.

Although, over the years, I have spent many hours browsing the aisles of my local GameStop—I was, after all, a video game junkie during my twenties, came of age in the era of *Pac-Man* and *Donkey Kong*, and have an eleven-year-old who can name every character in *Fortnite* and *Roblox*—I can honestly say that I never expected to write a book that revolved around the company or, at least, the company's stock. Like many people around the world—trapped at home during the height of the pandemic—I watched the market turmoil that came to a head the week of January 25, 2021, with a mixture of amazement and amusement. There was no question that something dramatic was happening: a David versus Goliath story involving a ragtag group of amateur investors, gamers, and Internet trolls taking on one of the biggest hedge funds on Wall Street. But it wasn't until I delved deeper into the story that I began to think that it was also something significant; that what we were all seeing, from our quarantine couches and our masked-up, socially distanced perches, was the first shot in a revolution—one that threatens to upend the financial establishment as we know it.

The deeper I looked, the more I believed—the battle that drove the price of a single share of GameStop to a pre-market high of $500 on January 28 had origins that dated back to Occupy Wall Street and beyond, when an anger toward big banks and the havoc wreaked in the last economic meltdown bubbled up into largely impotent protests and sit-ins. At the same time, the rise of GME could also be seen as the culmination of a populist movement that began with the intersection of social media and the growth of simplified, democratizing financial portals—tech that weakened the old-world pillars propping up the financial establishment, represented by the biggest upstart in the business, Robinhood, and its millions of mostly millennial devotees.

What seems certain, to me, is that this first, revolutionary shot—fired directly at Wall Street, if not from Main Street, from the basement of an amateur trader a few blocks away—is only the beginning. Those old-world pillars—protecting the suits and ties from the rabble outside—no longer seem so firm. A sea change has begun, right alongside the crypto revolution, with very similar philosophical implications.

It's impossible to know where this change will lead; how Wall Street will respond, whether what has now been unleashed by social media can even be contained. But historically, revolutions fed by anger tend to go in the same direction. At some point, once the pillars start to shake, the walls inevitably fall.

THE ANTISOCIAL NETWORK

PART ONE

There's deep value, then there's deep
fucking value.

—Keith Gill

CHAPTER ONE

January 26, 2021

Eight minutes past four in the afternoon.

A glass-walled office on the twenty-second floor of a skyscraper on Madison Avenue. Desolate, vacant, the lights dimmed, the empty trading desks lined up and lifeless, like high-tech terra-cotta soldiers, chairs pushed in, and Bloomberg terminals dark. A place that, one year earlier, would have been brimming with activity; the pulsing, beating heart at the center of one of the most powerful and successful hedge funds in the world. Now, quiet—along with all the other offices in all the other skyscrapers in the pincushion that was New York.

Twelve hundred miles away, tethered to that slumbering core by a somehow still functioning circulatory system of cell towers, satellites, and fiber-optic cables, Gabe Plotkin's world was coming to an end.

This can't be happening.

His tailored Oxford shirt was soaked through, and his tie felt like a noose around his neck, shifting up and down with each exaggerated throb of his rapidly accelerating pulse. His jacket was already off, draped over a corner of his chair, but it didn't make any difference. If he had been at his desk in that office on Madison Avenue, instead of lodged in an extra bedroom in his rented pandemic home in Florida, it would have been thirty degrees outside the picture window behind him—the kind of view generally reserved for Wall Street bankers, still staggering despite the sparse traffic snaking through the pincushion of Midtown and between the Covid-emptied sidewalks—and he'd have turned the heat as far down as it would go.

But here in Florida, the rivulets of sweat ran down the back of his neck and dampened the seams of his brightly patterned socks.

Impossible.

Gabe's eyes watered as he stared at the computer screen in front of him. The chart on the screen was inconceivable—and yet, there it was, a daggered mountain that rose like Everest where no mountain should have existed. Even as he watched, seconds ticking away at the bottom of the screen, charting the first few minutes of after-hours trading on an otherwise unremarkable Tuesday afternoon—that mountain was growing right in front of his eyes, *exponentially*, steeper and steeper, threatening to burst right out of the top of the goddamn screen.

Disastrous.

Gabe leaned back against his chair, bewildered. He'd seen trades go south before; hell, he'd been in the business long enough to know that the truly successful firms were defined by how they dealt with failed positions, not how they celebrated when things went right. Like any good trader, he'd learned that lesson the hard way.

Fourteen years ago, Gabe had been a fresh hire at Steve

Cohen's S.A.C. Capital Advisers—at the time one of Wall Street's most storied financial behemoths, $16 billion under management. The highest-returning hedge fund of its era—before becoming embroiled in an insider trading scandal in 2013. At S.A.C., Gabe had spent the first half of 2007 on a meteoric run, turning a $450 million bankroll into a $1 billion treasure chest, marking him as one of the hottest traders on the street. S.A.C. had begun handing him more and more money to invest—when just as suddenly, Gabe's positions had teetered and crashed. By the end of that summer, he'd lost 80 percent of his investments. It had been an existential moment—many traders would have packed it in. But Gabe had been resilient. He'd picked himself up, wiped the blood from his nose, put a frozen steak against his bruised and beaten eyes. He'd learned to rely on his process, continually reassessing his positions in a rapidly changing environment. By the end of that year, he'd made back every penny he'd lost, and then some.

Over the next six years, he'd grown into one of the top traders at S.A.C. In the fallout of the SEC investigation that had turned S.A.C. inside out—leaving Steve Cohen himself mostly untouched but sending a couple of his traders to prison—it had come time for Gabe to open up his own shop. He'd promptly raised $1 billion, part of it from Cohen's new manifestation, Point72, and after that, Gabe had never looked back. He'd built a diverse team of the right people, who could trade at the highest levels, humble but willing to work hard.

Eight years later, Melvin Capital was now one of the brightest lights on the Street. From its inception in 2014, Melvin had achieved annual returns of 30 percent all the way through 2020; in 2020, the firm was up 52.5 percent net. Gabe's star had gone supernova; he'd personally earned, reportedly, over $800 million last year alone, and was rapidly collecting the accoutrements of his growing station at the top of the banking hegemony. There was the minority ownership in a professional sports team, the Charlotte Hornets, which made him partners with Michael Jordan—*Michael Jordan!*—one of his childhood idols. A lavish apartment on the East Side, and of course, there was even the Miami waterfront mansion. Actually, the one mansion hadn't been big enough, so he'd bought two mansions next to each other for $44 million, intending to knock one down to make room for a tennis court, a cabana, and a kids' playground. The place had come complete with a private dock, which meant Gabe would certainly need a boat, because what good was a dock without a boat? For that matter, what self-respecting hedge fund titan with $13 billion under management didn't have a boat?

But staring at the screen and that digital Everest spiking upward, pixel after nauseating pixel, thoughts of palaces in Miami, pickup basketball games with Michael Jordan, and pitifully boatless private docks were far from Gabe's mind.

What he was seeing wasn't possible, and yet it was unmistakable: despite all logic and reason, despite months of intense research, despite many soul-crushing hours spent sifting through financial reports and on phone calls with analysts and experts—he was about to be handed the biggest loss of his career.

A loss so large, it might destroy everything he had built—and bigger than that, Gabe worried, it would sound an alarm bell that would clang through all of Wall Street, with ramifications that would be felt for years to come.

Gabe's Melvin Capital, which he'd named after his grand-father, a convenience store owner, one of the most honest, hardworking men he'd ever known—had reportedly lost nearly $5 billion in a matter of days—much of it in the *last twenty-four hours*. All of it, on a single stock, of a company that was almost too ludicrous to name. A stock that should have been crashing, but instead was flying through the roof.

Gabe, one of the most powerful men on Wall Street, had just been bested by some unseen force. Something, he would soon learn, that was growing in the deepest, darkest corners of social media—a revolution, firing its very first shot across the establishment's bow. And perhaps the biggest indignity of it all—the coup de grâce had been delivered by a single tweet just minutes ago, from the biggest troll on the entire Internet.

Gabe closed his eyes. Thoughts of boats, Jordan, Miami flickered and tangled up like images on a strip of film that had come unhoused from the projector. He took a deep breath and turned the computer off.

Then he reached for his phone.

CHAPTER TWO

December 2020

Six weeks earlier and four hundred miles away, Jeremy Poe, twenty-two years old and built like a wire hanger that had been untangled and extended to break in through the crease in the window of a locked car, stood by himself at an institutional-style metal table at the front of the vast Presidential Ballroom of the Washington Duke Inn and Golf Club, wondering how in the hell it had all come to this.

The only thing he knew for sure was that this wasn't what his senior year of college was supposed to be like. He'd seen all the movies, read all the brochures. Senior year was supposed to be barhopping and keg parties, class dances, maybe a romance or two, afternoons hanging out on the Quad, and bull sessions in his dorm room that went on all night, until the morning light streamed in through his window and his alarm went off, telling him he was late for class—but who cared, really, because it was senior year, the last gasp before college ended and the real world came roaring in.

Instead, he was standing in a gigantic ballroom along with a dozen of his classmates, lined up in staggered, socially distanced lines beneath elegant chandeliers dripping tear-drops of crystal. Each kid, like him, waiting for a turn at that frighteningly sterile steel table cluttered with vials, specimen bottles, and sanitizing lotion.

There was a nurse a few feet away, watching Jeremy with eyes that might have been blue, but just as easily could have been green. At least Jeremy thought she was a nurse; she was wearing a mask and a face shield and rubber gloves, but then again, so were a lot of people inside the ballroom, and also out on campus and in the streets of Durham and, for that matter, on TV and in the newspapers and just about everywhere else. *High fashion in the age of Covid.* But this woman also had on scrubs, which meant she probably knew what she was doing. And despite the way the light from the chandeliers splashed obscuring patterns across her face shield, Jeremy could see the impatience in her blue or green or blue-green eyes.

Jeremy offered an apologetic smile as he readied himself for the task ahead. He wasn't wearing a face shield, and his own mask was down under his chin—but only because of the thing he held in his right hand. Six inches long and topped with an evil-looking wisp of cotton. A cruel twist on the party skewer, and to Jeremy's thinking, this was about as far from a party as a college senior could get.

At least the ballroom itself was mildly festive; the carpet beneath his feet was lush and ornately patterned in reds and blues, and there were thick velvet drapes surrounding the many windows that looked out onto one of North Carolina's premier golf courses. And of course, there were those chandeliers, sprouting from the ridiculously high ceiling like frozen, sparkly jellyfish, glistening tendrils waving in the breeze from the specially designed air circulators that had been set around the perimeter of the room.

"Nothing to it," the nurse said, her voice muffled by her mask. "Just stick it in your nostril, give it a few turns, and leave it in the specimen container on the table."

Jeremy tried to think of something witty to say back, but then decided that the moment wasn't right. It was hard to be suave when you were about to stick something up your nose. Sure, this was better than the test they used to use, back in the spring before the campus had shut down when Covid first hit. *That* damn swab had been twice as long and had seemed to go right up into your brain.

Truth be told, Jeremy was usually pretty good at small talk and making people laugh; he probably would have had a chance of at least getting a positive reaction out of the nurse if he had been holding a cocktail skewer instead of a nostril-bound swab. Then again, though he wasn't shy, he was quirky, with an idiosyncratic personality; although he'd made a few good friends over his first three years at Duke, he had really been looking forward to senior year to build on that social framework, bust out in a bigger way.

When he thought about it, he knew the quirkiness wasn't entirely his fault. His upbringing had been, in a word, unique. Not a lot of kids could say they'd grown up on a boat, bouncing along the coast of Florida when he wasn't zigzagging between various Caribbean islands. For much of his childhood, his morning commute had involved tide charts and docking fees, and his only real companions had been his family—his dad and mom and his younger brother, Casper. You didn't gain many normal social skills on a 44-foot catamaran, and by the time he'd hit junior high and entered a regular school, he'd already developed some eccentric habits. But he'd put in a lot of work on his personality since then and gotten much of his anxieties and social awkwardness under control.

Still, under the most ideal of circumstances, it was always hard breaking the ice with strangers, and this particular circumstance was far from ideal. At the moment, the best he could manage was an amiable smile.

He couldn't tell if the nurse smiled back, because of the mask, but he took it for a win. Then he turned his attention back to the swab, stuck it in his nose, and gave it a confident twist.

*　　*　　*

Twenty minutes later, Jeremy's nostril was still stinging as he shook the remnants of a hard drizzle from his hooded sweatshirt, kicking his sneakers off in the foyer of his economical one-bedroom, off-campus apartment. The Dunworthy Pines, a sprawling complex of multistory residences on the south side of Durham, wasn't anywhere near as flashy as its name, which made Jeremy think of a daytime soap opera—pretty people playing out dramatic storylines while congregating in bikinis and Speedos around a lavish communal swimming pool. But it wasn't entirely awful. There was indeed a swimming pool, and even a man-made lake, both of which Jeremy could have seen through the sliding glass doors on the far end of his living room if the shades hadn't been currently drawn. And the grounds around the lake were fairly manicured, a maze of low bushes and pruned trees crisscrossed by cobbled and stone paths designed for walking. Though the Pines was teeming with college kids who, like Jeremy, had opted to avoid the cramped accommodations of the college's main campus, there wasn't any congregating going on, at least that he was aware of. It was mostly strangers sharing hallways, everyone hiding behind masks and invisible six-foot repulsion fields, doing their damned best to keep to themselves.

When Jeremy had first arrived on campus, he'd been pretty lonely—which was saying a lot for a kid who'd grown up on a boat. But then at his father's urging, he'd taken the initiative to create a bubble with a few of his classmates who happened to live in the same complex. Karl, two floors above Jeremy, was one of his best friends at Duke, a biology major and martial arts hobbyist who taught Jeremy both how to wrestle and how to better maintain a healthy lifestyle, helping him keep himself physically fit despite how focused he was on academics. Karl's girlfriend, Josie, who was a better wrestler than either Jeremy or Karl, studied applied math and political science. And a third classmate, Michael, whom Jeremy had met in his advanced linear algebra class, happened to share Jeremy's double major—math and psychology—which meant they had a joint penchant for making themselves miserable, coupled with a drive to figure out *why* they were chasing said misery. Between Jeremy's bubble, which got together twice a week, and his course load, which included such mouthfuls as *Bayesian statistics*, *probabilistic machine learning*, and the *cinema of psychopathology*, it was almost possible to forget that the outside world had come to a grinding halt.

Jeremy yanked his hood back as he moved deeper into his apartment, freeing his tangled mop of reddish hair, which sprang up above his high forehead like some sort of demented, rust-colored halo. He hadn't been to a barber since before Covid, though he had tried to take clippers to himself a handful of times over the past few months, to his own detriment. Then again, one of the benefits of a pandemic was that it didn't really matter how you looked, when most of your social life took place through a little square floating around the screen of your laptop. Zoom was the great equalizer, and a good, high-definition webcam beat a proper haircut every time.

Jeremy moved deeper into his apartment, pulling his cell phone out of his pocket as he went. A little green light on a speaker planted halfway up a set of bookshelves that separated the foyer from the living area told him the magic of Bluetooth was already two steps ahead of him, and with a flick of a finger, he coaxed the music app on his phone to life.

As usual, his playlist was cued up to his favorite song, and the first hyperkinetic chords of some seriously frenetic Japanese pop spiraled out at him from the speaker, like explosive ringlets of invisible, electronic confetti. Kanako Itō, of course, because for the past year or so it was almost always Kanako Itō. Her real name was Itō Kanako—in Japanese they put the last name first—one of the many things Jeremy had learned as his love for anime and, specifically, for a series called *Neon Genesis Evangelion*, had ballooned into a near obsession. Jeremy had consumed *Evangelion* in one marathon sitting after he'd been introduced to the midnineties Japanese TV production by a well-traveled cousin. The plot of the anime series—which had included manga, movies, and video games, on top of the twenty-six original episodes—was incredibly complex, involving a global apocalypse, enormous bio-robots battling even bigger monsters, mysticism, Judeo-Christian imagery, and lots of teenage angst. The series was made even more impenetrable by the fact that Jeremy had watched it all the first time through in the original Japanese, which he didn't speak; but even so, he had concluded that it was an absolute masterpiece, and he'd often posited that it was, in fact, a miracle that something that good had ever been made. He'd spent many hours trying to decode the story and its themes using every Internet source at his disposal—a journey that had led him even deeper into anime, where he'd discovered countless more series such as *Kaguya-sama: Love Is War*, *Kiki's Delivery Service*, and the *Science Adventure* series of visual novels, including *Steins;Gate* and *Robotics;Notes*, the latter of which he had binged—the whole forty hours' worth—in three or four days.

From the anime, it had been a short hop to the music; Kanako Itō, Kikuo, pop, and metal. At the end of his junior year, while writing a paper on algebraic number theory, he'd listened to a single Japanese metal album fifteen times in a row over the course of a week, during which he'd taken repeated breaks to dance, letting the music move him like a puppet to get his creative juices flowing.

At the moment, as he crossed his apartment toward the desk in the corner by the glass back doors, where his laptop computer waited, he wasn't dancing; but he did have his *Neon Genesis Evangelion* T-shirt on under his hoodie, and there was at least one book of manga on the desk's glass-and-chrome top by the laptop's keyboard.

The desk itself—shiny, sheer, glossy, with retractable legs and way too many wheeled feet—could have doubled for a mechanized battle robot in a pinch; Jeremy's brother, Casper, had put the damn thing together when Jeremy had first moved into the apartment. It was something that would have taken Jeremy a few days to accomplish, but Casper had finished the job in a short afternoon. Casper had always been the more practical minded of the pair, which was probably why he had chosen to major in civil engineering, while Jeremy had taken the more theoretical route. Which meant that although they were both focused on mathematics at the same university, separated only by two years, they'd barely crossed paths even before the pandemic.

Unlike Jeremy and despite Covid, Casper had chosen to experience his sophomore year from a dorm room on campus because he'd wanted to be closer to his friends. From what Jeremy had gleaned from the first few weeks of the fall semester—a barrage of quarantines, weekly testings, social distancing requirements—it didn't seem like Casper would have it much better than Jeremy, as isolated as he was. It hadn't taken long for Jeremy to realize—whether it was in a dorm surrounded by classmates, or in an apartment surrounded by strangers—a pandemic was something you went through alone.

As he lowered himself into the chair in front of his desk, he yanked his mask from his chin and tossed it toward a nearby garbage can. He missed by a good yard, the flicker of crumpled medical-grade paper landing next to a pile of dirty clothes. Sooner or later he'd cart the pile down to the shared laundry room in the basement of his complex; who knows, maybe he'd get lucky and someone would be at one of the other machines. Maybe he would have a conversation in person—an activity he vaguely remembered, involving a real interchange of thoughts turned into words, thoughts that might even have nothing to do with coronaviruses or the proper use of PPE or testing rituals, thoughts communicated without the use of computer software or a wireless router.

He smiled at the idea, then began to hit keys on his laptop, powering up the sleeping screen. To his right, beyond the collection of manga, stood an imposing stack of math textbooks, most with titles that would have terrified anyone he'd meet in a laundry room, even at a university like Duke. Next to the books, a pad of yellow-lined paper—the first few pages of which were already filled with the beginnings of a problem set that had been assigned even before school had returned to session. But at the moment, as his fingers danced across the keyboard, his thoughts were not on his homework, or the anime, or even friendly, imaginary strangers in equally imaginary, Covid-free conversations in less-than-imaginary laundry rooms.

Instead, his focus was on the laptop, which, since the start of his senior year, had pretty much become the center of his universe. Not just because it was where he would soon be attending his classes, and conducting much of his socializing. Apart from school and his existing network of friends and family, he'd recently discovered a new endeavor, which was taking up more and more of his time. An interest that had started as a curiosity had progressed to something of a hobby, and was rapidly becoming another of his obsessions, right alongside his passions for anime, Japanese pop, and anxiety-inducing introspection.

While he continued to hit keys on the keyboard, he once again removed his phone from his pocket, and placed it on top of the book of manga. A deft flick of his thumb shifted the phone's screen from his music library to a different app—the display turning an instantly appealing, leafy shade of green, broken only by an image a third of the way from the top—a feather, as if floating down from above the phone, plucked from the brim of some fairy-tale character's hat.

Something about that image always made Jeremy's adrenaline kick in; he assumed the reaction was Pavlovian, involving a minute dopamine hit from some overcharged structure in his brain. He had no doubt that the people who had designed that screen had spent hours contemplating colors, shades, and pictures—he'd read somewhere that casinos employed dozens of scientists when they designed their gaming halls, to find the perfect blend of lighting, materials, decorations, even scents—to engage their customers on a subliminal, primal level. He had no idea if the people behind the app on his phone had gone to similar lengths in building their home screen—all he knew for sure was that a glance at his phone hit him like the first chords of his favorite Kanako Itō.

But before he gave in to the sudden urge he had to shift past that home screen and deeper into the app, he turned his attention back to his laptop. In the few moments since he'd sat at his desk, he'd already scrolled past his e-mails, pushed aside a couple of Word documents and a math project in progress. Now dominating the center of the screen was something else—and the minute his eyes began scanning along, he found that he was grinning.

Jeremy knew that In Real Life, he could be more than a little quirky, and sometimes self-limiting in his interactions with others. Pastimes like theoretical math, anime, and a healthy fear of Covid didn't lend themselves to developing much of an overly large friend network. But trapped in his apartment, with his Japanese pop blaring and his math homework piling up, he had recently found something else to take its place. That screen in front of him was no longer some two-dimensional tool to connect him to places and people he used to visit and see. It had become a portal to an entirely new community—one that was becoming more real and encompassing, even as the actual world became more bizarre and unsocial day by day.

He leaned forward, scanning the screen, as his smile grew.

"Okay, fellow apes and retards," he whispered to himself. "What do you have for me today?"

CHAPTER THREE

Wilmington, Massachusetts.

A little before six on a frigid night, the kind of New England evening where the air was so cold, you could see the wind as much as feel it. A pretty street tucked into the corner of a leafy, sleepy suburb, twenty minutes along the commuter rail from downtown Boston.

The kind of place where you closed your eyes and twenty years flashed past.

Keith Gill, thirty-four, with high cheekbones, piercing brown-hazel eyes, and a magnificent mane of shoulder-length hair that perhaps tended toward mullet when you saw it from the side, stood in the frozen grass of his postcard-sized lawn, straining his arms to lift his two-year-old daughter onto the top of the plastic slide that squatted in the shadow of his three-bedroom home. His daughter was smiling in the way only a two-year-old on the top of a slide could smile—an expression of pure joy tinged with anticipation, without the slightest hint of fear. She just wanted to slip over that edge and go fast, faster, as *fast as she could*.

No doubt she got that from her father. For as long as Keith could remember, he'd been fast—and striving to go faster. Even now, midway into his thirties, every cell in him felt the spark of that dormant kinetic energy. When he was a kid, the hardest thing in the world had been to sit still; earlier than he could even remember, he'd funneled that bottled-up drive into running. He'd just point himself in a direction and go—and by the age of twelve, he'd already made a name for himself as the fastest kid in his neighborhood.

It had been a different suburb then: Keith had grown up in Brockton, a more working-class version of Wilmington, one of three children to a father who drove a truck for a living and a mother who worked as a registered nurse. Brockton wasn't rich or fancy or pretty, but it was proud as hell, the kind of place that only looked over its shoulder long enough to land a good elbow. A place cocky enough to call itself "the city of champions," refusing to give up the title even after nearby Boston and its longtime Mayor Menino pointed out that all the championship parades ran down Boylston Street, not Route 28. Tom Brady was the GOAT and guys like Bourque and Bird and Ortiz could make miracles, but anyone from Brockton could tell you where the real champions were from. Guys like Rocky Marciano and Marvin Hagler, who worked their way up from public high schools; and right there alongside them was Keith Gill, gravitating to track because he wasn't quite good enough for pro baseball or big enough to play football or mean enough to play hockey. And besides, damn it, he was *fast*.

In short order, the fastest kid in the neighborhood became the fastest kid in his hometown. Then he was the fastest kid at Brockton High School, and by the time he matriculated to nearby Stonehill College, he was known as one of the top racing prospects in the state. At Stonehill, the records had continued to accumulate: He ran the indoor 800 at 1:52. The 1000-meter at a hair above 2:24. And a 4.03 mile, which put him in the elite of college runners. Fewer than 1500 people in the world had broken a four-minute mile, and Keith was just a few breaths away—earning himself the title of Division II Indoor Athlete of the Year, and landing himself, along with his track-racing brother, Kevin, in the pages of *Sports Illustrated*.

If it hadn't been for a combination of serious injuries involving his Achilles tendon and a lingering bout of mono, there was no telling where Keith's innate speed would have taken him. He might even have been able to follow his dream and pursue a professional track career. Then again, Keith was fully aware that track wasn't football or hockey. You didn't retire rich from running fast.

Keith took another breath of the frigid air and stepped back to watch his daughter as she tilted forward then took off down the cold plastic slide. Her squeal cut through the night air, making Keith smile. He could see his wife, Caroline, through the first-floor window that looked in on their compact kitchen, and she was smiling, too.

It wasn't a four-minute mile—but a guy like him growing up where he had grown up could have done a lot worse than the quiet, simple life he'd built for himself. A home— rented, to be sure, but still—a wife, a kid, a job. Maybe not a dream job—hell, nobody dreamed about working for what some might call a second-tier insurance company like Mass Mutual, and certainly nobody fantasized about what Keith actually did day to day, which was to develop financial education classes that financial advisors—people who made twice as much as Keith, who had gone to better colleges, and probably had grown up to richer parents, but no way in hell could have run anywhere near a four-minute mile—could present to prospective clients.

Keith himself wasn't entirely sure how he himself had ended up at Mass Mutual. Bottom line was, 2009 had not been the best year to be graduating from college and looking for a job. Despite the fact that he was the first in his family to earn a four-year degree, graduating from Stonehill hadn't exactly thrown open the doors to an easy future. A kid from Brockton with few connections didn't have a ton of options, and being so close to Boston had as many disadvantages as advantages. Competing with brainiacs from Harvard and Tufts and the rich kids from BU for the handful of available positions hadn't been easy—from 2009 to 2017, Keith had spent much of his time unemployed. When he'd gotten the job at Mass Mutual at the beginning of 2019, he'd been completely out of work for the better part of two years.

It wasn't a dream situation, but it did put food on the table, and as he told himself every day—prepandemic—when he'd strapped on a tie and fought the traffic on 93 to Mass Mutual's offices, it *was* a job in finance. As a kid, he'd always been good with numbers, and he loved looking for edges that other people didn't see. His mother often told a story about how he'd search the streets and sidewalks for scratch tickets people had thrown away, hoping to find jackpots the people who'd bought the tickets hadn't noticed. By college, that had morphed into an ability to do deep research—again, always looking for something other people had somehow missed. Track had taught him how to work hard and to push himself—innate speed mattered, but you won races by digging deeper than everyone else—so by the time he'd graduated, he'd assumed finance would somehow be in his future. But he was also a realist; the investment banks weren't exactly knocking down doors in Brockton looking for the next Warren Buffett.

A short-term stint at a friend's start-up, followed by some finance work in New Hampshire in 2017, had gotten him to his Series 6 exam, which he'd passed easily to gain a trading license. And that, in turn, had gotten him to Mass Mutual. Prepandemic, he'd had an office—well, a shared space—but there were walls and a window, so it technically beat a cubicle. Maybe a couple years down the line, if he was lucky, he'd find his way onto a trading floor.

And even when Covid hit, and the office had shut down, and he'd traded the suit for sweatpants and his commute down 93 to a short stumble to the laptop on his kitchen table, he still considered himself lucky to have a job in finance. He knew a lot of people who had it a lot worse.

As his daughter reached the bottom of the slide, he lifted her up with both hands, high into the air. She was laughing, he was laughing, neither one of them gave a damn about the chill in the air—and yet, somewhere deep inside, Keith still felt that old kinetic spark. Deep down, he still remembered what it was like to be the fastest kid in his neighborhood, the kid who broke records, the kid who got to the finish line first.

It was a feeling he wasn't quite ready to put aside.

* * *

Four hours later, that kinetic feeling was still there as Keith descended the steps to the basement of his three-story home. Upstairs, Caroline was putting his daughter to bed, the dinner table was cleared, the dishwasher was churning away, leaking rivulets of soapy water onto the kitchen floor, something Keith would probably have to fix himself because it was ridiculously hard to get someone who knew anything about dishwashers into your house during a pandemic—but at the moment none of that mattered.

He stepped off the last step and into his basement, which was mostly finished, if more than a little sparse. There were kids' toys on shelves along one wall, boxes filled with games and puzzles in a cabinet by the stairs; but the small room at the back of the low-ceilinged space was all his. When they'd first moved into the house, he'd had a desk upstairs, with a window overlooking the neighborhood; but it hadn't been long before his daughter's finicky sleeping habits had banished him to the basement.

Three long steps, and he was through the door into what he jokingly referred to as his "kitty corner." One of his daughter's stuffed animals—a cat, of course, because in his house it was all about cats—was perched on the inner doorknob, and there was a poster of a cat hanging by its paws attached to the back wall; beneath the cat, the painfully banal quote: "Hang in there!" It wasn't the only cat poster Keith owned; he had similar posters rolled up and rubber banded together stored in one of the cabinets across the basement, along with a couple of cat-themed calendars and other feline-related paraphernalia, such as mugs, baseball hats, and more T-shirts than he'd want to admit. At the moment, he was wearing one of those shirts—emblazoned with a cat wearing dark aviator glasses, superimposed above a pair of fighter jets.

In front of the poster was his desk, supporting three large computer monitors as well as his laptop and a Bluetoothed keyboard. It was a fairly sophisticated setup, made even more impressive by the large, articulated microphone hanging above the desktop, painted a deep shade of crimson, which matched his even more imposing chair—made by the high-end gaming outfit Secret Lab, crafted in PU leather with black suede trim. The chair was a limited-edition, high-backed, adjustable design sporting the crest from House Lannister from the HBO show *Game of Thrones*, which was, of course, a lion, done in gold. The chair had cost Keith a small fortune, and Caroline had raised both eyebrows when it had arrived via UPS; but in the end, it seemed a small indulgence. Much of what he'd spent on the chair had been made up for by the cut-rate video streaming system he'd set up facing his workstation, and the mostly freeware editing software he'd added to his laptop's hard drive.

Keith lowered himself into the chair, mentally preparing himself for the evening ahead. Behind him, affixed to the wall behind the cat poster, was a rectangular white projection screen, which could double as a digital whiteboard. When the camera was going, his laptop often filled the board with notations, flow charts, calculations, and trading statements, though for the moment, the board was blank. Although he had an overall plan for the evening's broadcast, these things usually took on a life of their own.

Once that camera went on, Keith liked to let that kinetic energy take over. Which meant even *he* had no idea where he'd end up. By day, he was a mild-mannered suburban dad, who worked at an insurance company and taught advisors how to sell stocks. But down in his basement—he could become *someone else*.

He took a deep breath as he surveyed the rest of his desk's surface, making sure the accoutrements he'd need for his broadcast were where they were supposed to be. Closest to his keyboard was an Uno deck, and next to the brightly colored numbered cards, a red bandanna, currently resting around the neck of an unopened bottle of craft beer. Next to the bandanna and the beer, his Magic 8-Ball. The toy was stupid and very eighties—a shiny black sphere you would shake, with a little window that gave words of advice. When Keith was a kid, he'd ask it about girls, sports scores, things like that. The ball hadn't known very much about girls, even less about sports; but when you didn't like the answer it gave, you could always keep shaking until it told you what you wanted to hear. In practice, it wasn't all that different from the way most people at his day job picked the stocks they were selling to their customers. If a stock's chart didn't look good at first glance, turn it upside down; there was always a way to convince someone to buy.

He leaned forward and coaxed the computer screens to life. On the closest screen was his current portfolio, the various lines indicating the different stocks he'd purchased through a variety of online brokerages—none connected to the company where he worked. Along with straight equities, there were a handful of more sophisticated entities—mostly option calls, to extend his leverage, since he hadn't been working with much of a starting bankroll. Months ago, when he'd first begun livestreaming himself at his trading desk, his portfolio had been varied; but in recent months a single equity had dominated his computer screens, and to be fair, more and more of his life.

When he'd first launched his basement production, he hadn't intended to focus on a single equity, and he certainly hadn't predicted that the few-minute snippets of video would morph into many-hours-long livestreams, or that he'd be spending hours in his trading lair, sometimes late into the night, sometimes much of an afternoon. It had all started pretty simple: a YouTube channel under the persona "Roaring Kitty," built around Keith's passion for financial education. His goal had been to make short video segments explaining his mostly self-taught trading strategies, which revolved around finding value that other people had missed. His methods had to do with targeted research, which he approached much the same way he'd approached competitive running. Hard work, attention to detail, and almost delusional optimism.

The YouTube channel had been accompanied by a Twitter account, as well as regular posts on Reddit, under a more "Reddit-appropriate" handle, DeepFuckingValue. The name was another nod toward his trading philosophies—it was the *deep* value that made something worthwhile, even if you had to shake the 8-Ball a few times before you saw it.

And though he wasn't exactly becoming an Internet star—by the end of the summer, beginning of fall, his YouTube channel had amassed a few hundred followers at best—he'd found the experience surprisingly fulfilling. Like the rest of the world, he'd been thrown a curve by the pandemic, and suddenly here was a way to interact, show a bit of himself to a group of like-minded people, a few of whom maybe shared his sensibilities, his sense of humor, and perhaps even his trading strategies.

He was pretty sure Caroline understood—the livestreams, the posts, the camera—it was an outlet that took him right back to those days when he was a competitive runner. Like with running, trading was all about preparation. Digging deep, building a strategy, figuring out who you were up against. And then, when you were ready—you made your move.

Back in college, when Keith ran competitively, there was this feeling that the entire world was watching. Maybe it was mostly in Keith's head, but that was the real thrill: the wind whipping by and the crowd roaring, all those eyes watching what you could do. There was always this moment when the adrenaline was pumping, and your muscles were firing, and your mind became ridiculously clear. You felt like you were moving on air.

Maybe it was stupid; maybe nobody was really watching. But Keith had finally found, in some small way, something that duplicated that feeling.

He reached between the 8-Ball and the stack of cards, retrieved his bandanna from the neck of the beer, and tied it around his head. Then he hit a key on his laptop, faced his computer screens, exhaled—

As the camera

flicked

on.

CHAPTER FOUR

onna be one of those nights."

Kim Campbell looked up from her decaf, toward her colleague sitting two seats away down the waist-high desk that ran through the middle of their shared nurses' station. Chinwe—a head taller than Kim, dark-skinned beneath his navy blue scrubs, with a posture as upright, rigid, and proud as his personality—was gesturing toward the thick safety glass partition separating them from the dayroom. Even before Kim looked, she could tell he was right. Chinwe was usually right; one of the most experienced RNs on their unit, he had the work ethic befitting his first-generation immigrant status. There was very little that happened around the Davis Center of Psychiatric Medicine of which he wasn't aware. But at the moment, Kim hadn't needed Chinwe to know something was off. Six years since she'd taken her nursing position at the DCPM, she'd acquired a second feel for that sort of thing. Nursing was all about routine; it was the moments when the routine broke down, no matter how subtly, that made you wary.

The tension rose beneath her scrubs as she surveyed the brightly colored space on the other side of the safety glass; the dayroom was sparsely occupied, considering it was twenty minutes before shift change, which also happened to be medication time for a good portion of the patients who called the DCPM their temporary home. Usually, the two dozen or so residents would have been milling about the carpeted mixed-use area, some waiting patiently at the round tables situated along the far wall, others gathered around the seating area facing the TV—which was always turned to some innocuous game show or sitcom—anything without car horns or gun shots—the blander, the better. Kamal, another of her colleagues, was up at the medicine station, writing notes by the nearby whiteboard for the oncoming night shift; as usual, his notes were sparse and written so quickly that it would take a cryptographer to decipher them, something the next shift had gotten so used to, they called it "Kamal-lizing." When he was finished, Kim would take her own turn by the board, meticulously noting all the patients she had been caring for during her shift. A few that had been there since the night before, but mostly new arrivals, because the DCPM, being one of the premier mental health facilities in the area dedicated to involuntary admissions, was bustling during the best of times. Eight months into a pandemic, the place was bursting at the seams.

But strangely, tonight, Kim could see linoleum all the way to the pastel walls at the back of the room. The few patients that were nearby had moved off to the sides, and she was about to ask Chinwe what he thought was going on when she noticed the commotion at the rear of the carpet, right in front of the double doors leading deeper into the hospital.

Even through the thick partition she could hear the cursing, the agitated yelling. It was one of the newest arrivals, a man in his early sixties who'd been brought in late in the afternoon, skinny and leaning against a metal walker, probably drying out from something. Despite his fragile appearance, he had initially been designated by the sheriff a 5150, which meant, among other things, he was a danger to himself or others. Still, he wasn't restrained, which meant he'd calmed down enough from whatever he'd been on to safely join the general population.

The two orderlies who normally oversaw the room were on either side of him, talking in calm voices, trying to settle the man down—and even from a distance, Kim could see the stress in their eyes.

It took a certain personality to work in this area of health care; by definition, you were seeing people at the worst moments of their lives. Kim's own shifts ran twelve hours a day, 7:00 a.m. to 7:00 p.m., and she was just one of a full shift of four registered nurses, along with the orderlies and the two doctors who roamed the unit, admitting the new arrivals through the emergency room and monitoring the patients throughout the day.

The unit was locked, but the patients were free to come and go between the dayroom, the dining area, a separate rec room, and their semiprivate bedrooms. In total, Kim and her colleagues oversaw twenty beds on the floor, and another ten in the ER. The beds were almost always full, and like the man with the walker, none of the patients were there by choice. Many arrived in handcuffs, while others were brought in by ambulances or family.

When Kim had first graduated from nursing school a

decade earlier, she hadn't expected to end up in psych; she'd been focusing on emergency room nursing when she'd volunteered for a stint at a summer camp specializing in developmental issues and mental health. She'd found she had a real affinity for talking to people and a soft spot for people going through tough times. More than that, she'd realized, she loved a good transformation.

Working at Davis could be demanding, but seeing people change for the better, often in a very short time, was extremely satisfying. Patients came in at intense lows in their lives, often having just attempted suicide, or hitting some sort of drug-related bottom—and they usually left in a better place than when they came in.

On top of that, Kim found working in a psych unit more freeing than the other nursing disciplines she'd studied in nursing school. As her colleagues had quickly learned, she'd never had much of a filter, and a psych unit was one of the few places where that could be a real benefit. Connecting with the sort of patients Kim saw on a regular basis often took a mixture of straight talk and a strong sense of humor. You needed to be tough; when that ambulance opened its rear doors, you never knew whether you were going to get a college kid recovering from a self-inflicted gunshot wound or a homeless woman who'd been found wandering the freeway in her underwear or dancing on top of a car. They all came to Kim in pretty bad shape, and she had dedicated herself to trying to make them at least temporarily feel better.

From the looks of the rapidly devolving situation at the back of the dayroom, it seemed like DCPM's newest arrival needed a bit of direction; if he wasn't ready to smile at one of Kim's off-color jokes, a soft touch would probably do him a world of good.

She started up from the desk, which made Chinwe raise his eyebrows.

"I know," Kim said. "Ten minutes and it's night shift's problem. But my coffee's gone cold, so I figure, what the hell—"

It happened so fast, she never got a chance to finish the thought. The noise hit Kim first, a crack like a leather belt being pulled tight. And then came the safety glass, little bits raining down around her, shards bouncing off the nurses' desk like an icy rain. She looked over to see Chinwe on his feet, and a few yards over, Kamal, half covering himself by the whiteboard, pointing in shock—and then Kim saw it: the metal walker that the agitated patient had just been leaning against was now halfway imbedded into what was left of the partition that separated the nurses' station from the dayroom.

The patient was being restrained by the orderlies and was still shouting at the top of his lungs. Kim headed toward them, shaking remnants of glass from the sleeves of her scrubs as she went. Kamal saw her moving, and reached for a sedative they kept stored in one of the medicine cabinets behind the board; but as Kim came around the desk, she could see the sedative wouldn't be necessary.

Now that he'd gotten their attention, the man seemed to have mellowed, and was calmly talking to the security guards as they ushered him through the dayroom toward the double doors.

Kim turned back toward Chinwe.

"Ten minutes," he said. "Why do these things always happen right before shift change?"

Kim shook her head, breathing hard, as the broken glass crunched under her shoes.

*　*　*

A short time later, she was nursing a new cup of coffee as she sat at a round table in the nurses' break room, settling her thoughts. She still had some time before she needed to leave for her parents' house, to pick up her younger son before heading home to her three-bedroom apartment on the far side of town; her older son biked back and forth between her house and her ex's, which meant he wouldn't be blasting through the door until she was halfway done cooking dinner. She hadn't planned anything, so—spaghetti. That would most likely lead to a lot of complaining, because the older one was fifteen, and he'd spent the day cooped up at her ex's house enduring six hours of virtual school, which, as far as Kim could tell, was virtually useless.

So even though it had been a long day and there was still glass in her hair, she wasn't exactly in a rush to get home. She could at least finish her new coffee, which was on the table next to her open laptop. Her fingers were on the keyboard, but she wasn't typing, just scrolling. And the more she scrolled, the more the tension of the evening willowed away, the more her shoulders relaxed, the more she smiled.

Her expression must have been the first thing Chinwe saw as he pushed through the swinging doors from the hallway that led to the changing area. He'd traded his own scrubs for a pair of tan pants and a cardigan; he was always a snappy dresser, if a bit conservative—at the moment, he looked more like a college professor than an RN. Kim supposed it had to do with his background. She knew he was extremely well educated and had attended one of the top nursing schools after having immigrated to America from his native Nigeria. He was devoutly Christian and family oriented, and a big believer in right and wrong.

When they'd first met on the ward, they hadn't gotten along at all; Kim had a pretty big personality, and she could be crass and straightforward. In the beginning, many times she had inadvertently offended Chinwe's more parochial sensibilities. But over time, he'd realized that even her worst jibes came with a hefty dose of love, and they'd grown very close. Often, they referred to each other as "work husband and wife," though usually Kim designated herself as the "husband," and Chinwe as her antagonistic wife.

Dropping into the seat next to her, he was already shifting right into character, faux worry creasing the skin above his eyes.

"I'm scared to know what you're looking at."

Kim laughed, offering to shift the computer around so that he could see.

"Will I be offended?" he asked, cowering back.

"Definitely."

She was only partially kidding. Most of what she looked at online offended Chinwe, but to be fair, he could find something offensive in a Disney movie.

"Is it more right-wing baloney?"

She grinned—but shook her head. Chinwe wasn't alone in his distaste for her political leanings. He had been shocked—hell, all of her colleagues had been shocked—to discover that she had supported Trump in both elections. Though Kim was close to everyone on her staff—a mother bear to the other nurses, who were an extremely diverse group, covering every background and ethnicity one could imagine—they had all made it very clear that none of them understood how someone like her—educated, kind, compassionate, who had dedicated her life to helping others as a health care worker—could also be a Trump supporter. To be fair, even her own family had been shocked when she'd first admitted her leanings.

The many times she'd tried to explain it to Chinwe, he'd only looked at her with an expression that varied between pity and dismay. Growing up in a liberal community, she herself had never expected to fall for someone like Trump. She'd voted for Obama twice—but, she supposed, her current politics had risen in direct relation with the disappointments that had accumulated over the course of her adult life.

She knew some people would probably look at her as a walking cliché; a single mother of two who had been struggling to make ends meet since as long as she could remember, who had been let down by people, government, and life more times than she could relate. In 2008, she'd watched her parents almost lose their house in the financial crash. She herself had one failed marriage and two unexpected pregnancies. She'd liked Obama and what he'd represented—but really, what difference had he ever made in her life?

When Trump had come along, she'd immediately been attracted to his contrary nature; his shitposting, his assertiveness. He was different and seemed to piss people off, and she liked that about him. And what, really, did she have to lose?

She knew how upset it made people when they found out—and she'd taken a lot of heat from her coworkers during both election cycles. But she'd never been the type to keep her opinions to herself. She wore everything on her sleeves.

So of course, it was no surprise that Chinwe had hated her when they'd first met, and he'd never understand her support of Trump, who he considered racist and dangerous, and responsible for the fact that his adopted son was still unable to immigrate from Nigeria to be with him—but their friendship had advanced to the point where they could joke about it without any real animosity. On TV and outside on the street, politics could be polarizing. In the weeds of a psych ward, it was just a personality quirk, another thing to joke about during the long hours toward the end of a twelve-hour shift. In fact, on election day in 2016, Chinwe had bet Kim $100 that Hillary was going to win. When Trump had won, Chinwe had been so upset, he'd kept "forgetting" to pay. It had gotten to a point where a "frequent flyer" patient who knew about the bet would mention it every time he was hospitalized. Even now, though Trump had recently been voted out of office and Chinwe had earned back $100, the loss was a touchy subject, which Kim liked to bring up whenever she could.

"I promise," Kim said, pointing toward the computer. "It's not about politics."

Finally, Chinwe shifted forward in his seat and gave the screen his attention.

"WallStreetBets?" he read off the top of the screen. "What is this, a gambling site?"

Kim laughed.

"I guess, sort of. But no, it's a message board. On Reddit."

"Like, you write messages?"

"Sometimes, but mostly I read them."

Kim had stumbled onto the WSB board five years ago, entirely by accident. And truth be told, she *had* first gotten there because of her politics. She'd been on Reddit—the social media site that was basically a giant chat room broken up into boards catering to just about every hobby, political stance, belief, philosophy you could imagine—since right before the election of 2016. She'd been led there via Twitter, which she'd been on since 2014. And she'd gone to Reddit entirely because of Donald Trump. She'd discovered a board dedicated to Trump followers called r/The_Donald, which was basically a 24-7 Trump rally. Because of Reddit's belief in personal privacy—in stark contrast to sites such as Facebook—and the fact that the chat rooms, though moderated, allowed anonymous people to post almost anything they liked, under very loose content rules, from the very beginning r/The_Donald had been filled with over-the-top, contrarian dialogue, which then rapidly morphed into a chaotic hotbed of conspiracy theories, questionable speech, and an immense amount of verbalized anger. But despite the wildness of the Trump board, Kim had loved the community elements of being part of a conversation with people who at some level thought like her.

From the Trump board, she'd found her way to Wall-StreetBets. She hadn't known much about WSB's history but had learned a bit from reading posts. It had been founded by a thirty-year-old tech consultant named Jaime Rogozinski, who had wanted to build a forum for people who weren't cut from the conservative cloth regularly associated with Wall Street, to discuss stocks, investing, wins, and losses. From the very beginning, the site had catered to risk takers. The idea that Wall Street was, to many people, a glorified casino—that people often bought and sold stocks in the same way that others bet on horses, cards, or roulette wheels—wasn't unique to WSB, but perhaps the users who gravitated to WSB were more willing than anyone else to say so out loud. And unlike many other sites dedicated to talking about stocks, the WSB board was a place where people reveled in the misery of their losses—the bad buys that lost them their shirts—as often as they crowed about their wins.

Although Rogozinski had founded the site, he had eventually ended up getting removed from the very board he'd created when accusations surfaced—which he disputed—that he was trying to "monetize the sub" for personal gain. In his place, a variety of moderators had attempted to keep order over the years—a constant task, in the Wild West of one of the few truly anonymous corners of the Web.

When Kim had first stumbled onto the site, the moderator at the time had actually been Martin Shkreli—a hedge fund iconoclast, known in the media as the "Pharma Bro," who was pilloried for raising drug prices to obscene levels, purely for profit, and who eventually ended up in prison for securities fraud. Shkreli was just the sort of brazen, outspoken personality Kim found herself gravitating toward; even if she didn't respect what he stood for, she was intrigued by his wild, often unhinged personality.

The site itself, she had quickly realized, was a free-for-all; but it wasn't just idiots and amateurs talking about stocks.

A lot of the posters were day traders with experience and knowledge, and reading their posts was like taking a crash course in the stock market. And running beneath the constant conversation was something Kim recognized: an undercurrent of anger toward the rules that always seemed stacked against regular people like her.

She'd started visiting the site more and more, often reading the WSB board late at night, after she'd put her kids to bed. She loved that she was part of something that felt oddly conspiratorial. The WSB board was asking questions she herself could have articulated:

Why leave Wall Street to men in suits?

What had men in suits ever done for her?

And why the hell should men in suits have all the fun?

"What does this mean?" Chinwe asked, running his finger along the top of the screen, reading the small print an inch beneath the WallStreetBets logo/mascot, the image of a blond-haired trader in sunglasses and a suit and tie, like something out of an eighties video game—"'Like 4chan found a Bloomberg terminal.'"

Kim grinned. 4chan was one of the most notoriously dirty sites—a bulletin board, really—that bridged the gap between the dark web and more popular social media. And a Bloomberg terminal was what real Wall Street traders used to take money from regular people like her.

"It's kind of a motto. WallStreetBets is a place to talk about stocks, buying and selling."

"You mean investing."

"Sometimes. Sometimes gambling. Sometimes they're one and the same. The thing is, on this site, anything goes. The more subversive, the better."

Chinwe kept reading, and the wrinkles above his eyes grew deeper.

"There's a lot of bad stuff here."

Kim nodded. The moderators tried to keep the site relatively clean, but when you had a large number of anonymous people posting, sometimes you got ugliness. If Facebook was the model social network, WallStreetBets had a fierce antisocial tinge to it. The moderators didn't appear to be there to silence anyone—just to keep it somewhat civil.

The more Chinwe read, the more disturbed he seemed. A lot of the messages were wrapped up in pretty disgusting language. And many of them contained visual memes—video and pictures—that could get pretty blue. But Kim liked to think of the ugliness as sort of a smoke screen; it was a self-selection mechanism that kept the "suits" away. Guys who actually worked at Bloomberg terminals might be turned off by foul language and perverted memes. But regular folks who wanted to stick it to the suits? They'd found a home in the WSB board.

"'*Retards*,'" Chinwe read. "'*Apes.*'"

"Terms of endearment. It's mostly self-referential."

He looked at her, and she shrugged.

"If you keep reading, you'll see that some of the people on here are pretty sophisticated."

She leaned past him and scrolled to one of the messages. It was a deep dive into a particular equity, an analysis that went on for more than three paragraphs. It was the sort of research that no doubt had taken hours, maybe days, to compile. It made a pretty good case why the current price of a stock seemed undervalued to the poster, and why he was making a very big buy.

Beneath the text was an image—a screenshot from the poster's market account, showing what he had purchased.

Chinwe whistled.

"Is this real? This number—he spent that much? And then he posted it here? Why would he do this?"

She shrugged. In some ways, what went on within the WSB board was incredibly intimate. Almost as intimate as if these anonymous strangers had been writing about their sex lives. This was real money—or at least it appeared to be—and this guy was taking an enormous risk. And he was telling Kim about it, showing it to her, in real time. You didn't get more intimate than that.

"And you can buy stocks through this?"

"No. Here, you talk about them. To buy them, you have to go somewhere else."

She reached below the table and into her purse, which was on the floor by her sneakers. The same sneakers she wore all day, below her scrubs. Sometimes she changed into pumps before she got to her mother's place; and on very rare occasions, she exchanged them for heels, when she went out to meet one of the other nurses for a drink, or if her best friend, Angie, happened to be up from Pasadena. Most days, though, she'd had enough of breathing through masks at work to want to put a new one on to sit outside a restaurant and watch other masked people scurry by.

Besides, who needed a social life when you had an anti-social network?

She put the phone on the table between herself and Chinwe, then began pushing through her apps until she found the right one. Then she hit the image with a slightly chipped nail, turning her entire screen a single shade of green—save for the little feather floating a quarter way down from the top.

"What is this?" Chinwe asked. "A video game?"

"It's much cooler than a video game."

She opened the app, watched as Chinwe's eyes went wide.

"It's Wall Street, Chinwe."

Wall Street, simplified and digitized and shrunk down so small, you could fit it in your goddamn purse.

CHAPTER FIVE

Christ, *I hate unicorns*, Emma Jackson thought to herself as she tried to find a comfortable sitting position on the ultramodern sofa in the center of the vast waiting area of the shiny, absurdly modern, brand-spanking-new Menlo Park headquarters of one of the fastest-growing companies in Silicon Valley. It was a difficult task, considering that the sofa was way too short, which meant Emma's knees were almost to her shoulders. She'd never thought a piece of furniture could be pretentious before she'd started working with Valley Internet companies, but by her sixth year in the rapidly growing fintech industry, she'd visited enough headquarters to know that anything—and she really meant *anything*—could be pretentious.

Windows could be pretentious—like the enormous, twenty-foot-high ones that doubled as walls, surrounding the open waiting area where she was seated. Ceilings could be pretentious, like the vaulted wooden one above her head, with its exposed beams and deep tones that would have been more suited for a ranch-style country estate or a fancy beach house than a tech company's lobby. Courtyards could be *terrifyingly* pretentious—like the one on the other side of those windows, paved in wood and cobbled in stone, complete with a fire pit surrounded by a phalanx of potted plants.

Even so, Emma supposed, the Menlo Park offices were a step up from the company's previous headquarters in Palo Alto, basically a carved-out shell squatting near a strip mall, just a stone's throw from where the two young unicorn foals had been roommates at Stanford, before they'd grown their rainbow-spewing horns. Those offices had been warren-like and undoubtedly lower-rent—and yet somehow, Emma had been just as intimidated when she'd visited, back in early 2016. Maybe her feelings of inadequacy had been triggered by the vast murals that had covered nearly every inch of the walls of the original offices. Drawn in green and silver hues, by a talented artist named Nigel Sussman, the floor-to-ceiling paintings had depicted scenes set in the fictional setting of Sherwood Forest, and had depicted the fanciful story of Robin Hood and his merry band told through characters that all happened to be cats.

The new Menlo Park offices had murals as well: more cats, but the merry band was now seen driving around in cars and floating through space and riding motorboats. Emma had to admit she preferred the original motif; at least it was on the nose, and either way, she didn't quite get the growing, Internet-fed infatuation with the feline species.

She supposed she was just being stuffy, showing her age with her outdated opinions on unicorns and cats. She was only thirty-nine, but at the moment she felt ancient. It didn't help that because of the open architecture of the waiting area, she couldn't avoid watching the two young entrepreneurs she had come to see, maybe a dozen yards away, halfway into a photo shoot in front of one of the many slabs of cat-infested wall. The photographer had already started on them when she'd first arrived, and the smiling assistant who had led her to the waiting area had offered her a cappuccino, which she'd politely declined. The last thing Emma needed was to try to juggle a steaming cappuccino while balancing on the damn couch, like some performer in Cirque du Soleil. So instead, she had nothing to distract her from the sight of the two impossibly young-looking men moving through awkward poses for the photographer, as a related journalist tossed them a stream of innocuous questions.

Emma wasn't sure which magazine or newspaper or blog or podcast the journalist was with: *BI*, the *WSJ*, the *Times*, hell, it could have been *Cat Fancy*. At the moment, the two prancing specimens in front of her were arguably the most sought-after magical creatures in the valley, even if the world at large was still mostly unfamiliar with them and their rapidly expanding company.

Vlad Tenev and Baiju Bhatt weren't household names, but their product was spreading through households and dorm rooms at an exponential rate, like a phone-born virus powered by pixie dust, exceptional design, and more than a little triggered greed. In just a handful of years since their inception, Robinhood was now well on their way to making true on their promise to upend the staid, direct-to-retail consumer banking industry—by putting the power of a Wall Street bank in the palms of anyone with a cell phone. On paper, Robinhood might have seemed like just another online brokerage—Schwab, Fidelity, E-Trade—but in practice, it was something else entirely. A disruptive, ingenious,

Jobs-like twist aimed directly at millennials and amateurs, a mobile portal to the stock market that was slicker than anything that had come before, as usable and compelling as a slot machine.

Emma watched as Vlad and Baiju tried their best to fulfill whatever vision the photographer was trying to convey. Vlad especially—but both of them, really—seemed so eager and accessible. Baiju gave off a warm, intellectual, spiritual vibe, with his wavy hair, scruff covering his jaw, a smile that was as charming as it was Cheshire. Vlad was more like a puppy dog or a stuffed animal, with eyes like a doe and long, straight hair that was more Prince Valiant than Robin of Locksley. Obviously, the two young men were best friends who shared a vision, and they didn't appear anywhere near as socially awkward as their résumés and origin story might have suggested. Then again, Emma had been in the business long enough to know that a good origin story had as much basis in reality as any other fairy tale. Still, every unicorn-led company had one, and Robinhood's was as storybook and accessible as a magical forest full of cats.

Emma had already heard much of the Robinhood myth since she'd arrived at the waiting area, parceled out in perfectly practiced answers—mostly from Vlad—to the soft-balls hurled by the fawning journalist. A fairy tale, for sure, Silicon Valley style: Vlad and Baiju had been two immigrant kids—Vlad from Bulgaria and Baiju from India—who had met as undergrads at Stanford, bonding over the fact that they were both only children of professorial parents, and that they shared majors in physics and math. In 2008, Vlad had matriculated to a graduate program at UCLA, planning to become a mathematician, while Baiju had gone to work at a trading firm near San Francisco. When the markets crashed later that year, spurred by the fall of Lehman, the massive investment bank, the best friends, on Baiju's urging, decided to pack their bags and chase the American dream. They'd headed east with the idea that they could use their mathematical skills to build a trading start-up to offer highly sophisticated tools to hedge funds and banks, who were clawing their way out of the turmoil by turning to automated strategies, to "trade ahead" of orders—flash trading, as it became known—which turned pennies made on large volumes of tiny spreads into billions of dollars.

But, the story went, Vlad and Baiju became increasingly unsettled by the notion that their business was basically helping rich people get richer; as market inequities and the resulting anger turned into the movement known as Occupy Wall Street—a mass protest of mostly the young and angry, who took to the streets of New York to agitate for change— the two friends began to question their role in helping hedge funds and bankers stomp all over retail traders. When one of Vlad's close friends went as far as to accuse him of "profiting" off the unfairness of the markets, he and Baiju had decided to try and use what they had learned, and the technology they had developed, to level the playing field.

They'd chosen the name "Robinhood" for obvious reasons; the medieval, mythical character Robin and his merry band of thieves had made it their mission to redistribute wealth, by stealing from the rich and giving to the poor. Vlad and Baiju built their own *mission statement* in allegorical style: instead of redistributing wealth, they would "democratize finance"—giving the retail traders Wall Street had spent a century steamrolling the necessary tools to fight back, on even ground. Robinhood's plan was simple and twofold: offer regular people commission-free trading and do away with minimum account balances. Furthermore, the company from the start would be built around the smartphone rather than the computer—because if there was one thing young people knew, loved, and trusted, it was that shiny little screen in their hand.

Emma blinked as the photographer's flash went off, catching Vlad and Baiju in a faux-casual moment of conversation. Of course, Vlad had his phone out of his pocket for the shot, no doubt open to the Robinhood app.

Even in her most jaded moments, Emma had to admit the app was beautiful. Vlad and Baiju had certainly built their portal with their audience in mind. Simple, slick, and addictive; opening an account was as easy as logging into Facebook, and once you'd transferred some funds—any funds—to your profile, you could trade equities with a push of a button. Search for any stock you liked, and the app brought you to a single page with all the information you might need: price; an instant chart showing daily, weekly, monthly, yearly change; volume—and a big fat button on the bottom just begging you to trade. The color scheme was gorgeous, and there were plenty of visual, auditory, and even tactile incentives along the way. Hell, when you made your first purchase, confetti rained down the screen. In Emma's opinion, they hadn't just leveled the playing field by giving the average Joe a sophisticated trading tool that fit in his pocket; they'd turned the entire stock market into a highly playable video game. And if there was one thing the millennials and college kids who gravitated toward Robinhood loved and intimately understood, it was video games.

Emma knew that the average age of a Robinhood user—a base that had passed 2 million by 2018 and would grow by a factor of 3, then double again in the next two years—was around thirty-two—but the median was much lower, somewhere in their twenties. And to Robinhood's credit, it was certainly mostly Main Street, not Wall Street, clicking those buttons and watching that confetti fly. They'd "democratized Wall Street," just as they'd promised. But what Main Street didn't realize was that democracy usually came at a cost. When you looked a little deeper, the fairy tale frayed at the edges, and Robinhood wasn't quite the bane of the rich as the myth might have led one to believe.

Emma shifted against the couch, willing her legs not to fall asleep, as she continued to wait for the photographer and the journalist to finish their work. No doubt, the pictures would come out great, and the magazine profile, newspaper article, or blog post would rave on about "disruption," "equality," maybe even "fairness." And that would all be true. But Emma knew better than most—the story was painfully incomplete. Because what was less obvious about the Robinhood story—what barely made it into the glowing stories and fairy tales—was how Robinhood actually made their money.

And who could blame the magazines? "Payment for order flow" was a mouthful, and it didn't make anywhere near as good copy as "democratizing finance." In simple terms, Robinhood was able to offer zero commissions because their users weren't actually their customers—they were, essentially, the *product*. Robinhood bundled up and sold their users' trades to market makers—giant financial firms such as Two Sigma, Susquehanna, but primarily Citadel—

who could near-instantly analyze the trading flow and profit by taking tiny slivers out of the spreads between bids and asks. Because Robinhood's main users were amateurs who made risky trades—and more and more, gravitated toward more leveraged and even riskier plays such as options—Robinhood could command a premium from the market makers, whose profits went even higher the more volatile the trading flow.

So the same people who had benefited from Vlad and Baiju's flash-trading software were now benefiting even more from Robinhood's "democratization of finance." Emma didn't fault them for their profits, nor did she fault Robinhood for the way they filled their coffers. She was a clear-eyed professional, who worked for a fund herself, after all. And Robinhood's users were getting to trade without commissions, so in theory, everyone won. It was the moments when theory chafed against practice that things became a little less crystal.

Another flash went off, reflecting off Vlad's almost plasticine eyes, and for a brief moment his gaze connected with Emma, and then he quickly glanced away. She didn't fault him for that, either; she was used to that reaction. No doubt her meeting with Vlad and Baiju would be short, and way less fun than a photo shoot. Unlike the journalist, she wasn't there to talk democracy or Occupy Wall Street or cats playing medieval dress-up. She wasn't from Silicon Valley, she was from Chicago, and she was there to talk nuts and bolts.

And as little as Vlad wanted to talk payment for order flow, he'd want to discuss her specialty even less. Not because it involved some uncomfortable truth that would be hard for the public to swallow about how Robinhood made its money; but because what Emma did for a living was, to an outsider, *torturously boring*.

Emma had no problem admitting it to anyone who asked: *clearing* was the least glamorous part of finance, and one that very few people actually understood—or ever wanted to understand. Like payment for order flow, it had to do with the piping behind how trading worked, and it was almost never talked about in cultured company. You'd never see an article in a glossy magazine about clearing, and nobody was asking Emma to pose in front of any murals.

But that didn't make what she did any less important, or what she had come to talk to Vlad and his team about any less imperative.

It wasn't the first time Emma had visited Robinhood to discuss clearing; in fact, when Robinhood had first opened its doors, Emma's bosses—through one of the companies in their portfolio, Apex Clearing—had helped launch the revolutionary brokerage, taking care of the "boring" side of the business so that the two unicorns could frolic unencumbered by worries of what might be flowing through the roots beneath their hooves.

She could still remember that initial meeting, when her bosses—Matt Hulsizer and Jenny Just, brilliant billionaires in their own rights who had built one of the most forward-thinking, if under-the-radar, fintech conglomerates in the world—had tried to explain, in as simple terms as possible, why it was vital that anyone trying to build a business in the banking space had to fundamentally understand clearing. Emma hadn't even needed to see how quickly Vlad's eyes had clouded over during that first meeting to know that their words were not hitting home. Vlad's vice president of Business Development had been standing on a skateboard through the entire presentation, and when Matt had off-handedly mentioned the "30s" rules that outlined how much money—separate from the trading money Robinhood took in from its users—the company would need to settle trades with the Federal Clearinghouse, the man had commented: "Twenty thirty? That's so far from now."

Matt had dutifully explained that the "30s" rules referred to the 1930s. Back in the 1930s, when many of the regulations surrounding the clearing of stock trades had been put into place, entrepreneurs who wanted to get into banking didn't stand on skateboards during meetings or have walls covered in murals showing cats with bows and arrows.

Everyone in the room had agreed: Robinhood's design was brilliant. But as Matt had put it at the time: "Vlad, you're Michelangelo, you're an artist—not an engineer. And this isn't some painting, some beautiful sculpture. This is a building. St. Peter's Basilica. If it falls down, people are going to get hurt."

But it had been obvious from the start, the adults in the room weren't going to get through to the unicorns. And it was little surprise that, a couple of years later, Robinhood made the decision to handle clearing in-house, by building out their own clearing division to act as an intermediary to the Federal Clearinghouse, which monitored all their trades. It was magical thinking at its best: you don't fully understand something that people are telling you is incredibly important, so you decide you can do it better yourself.

Now, two years later, Emma was back at Robinhood on behalf of her company to see if, perhaps, they'd want to revisit the conversation. But watching the two entrepreneurs as they finished their photo shoot—both of them barely giving her a glance, because she was probably about as interesting to them as the potted plants outside—she knew they weren't going to listen. They were going to continue to do this their way.

She didn't see any skateboards lying around, but it was clear to Emma that the unicorns were running Sherwood Forest—which was really more like Neverland, forever devoid of adult supervision. Besides, they probably thought—they hadn't built their app for the types of adults who'd want to supervise them anyway. And despite their business model and the way they actually made their money—they were adamant they hadn't built Robinhood for the fat cats at their trading desks on Wall Street, either.

Emma had to wonder—who, exactly, did they think they'd built Robinhood for?

CHAPTER SIX

Caledonia, Michigan.

The gray slog of 2:00 p.m.

Sara Morales stretched her tired calves against the vinyl footrest of a reclining chair in station three of the Shiny Locks Salon, as she leaned as far back as the cushioned headrest—and her own aching shoulders—would allow. Her phone rested gently on her stomach, rising and falling with each fatigued breath, but she could still see the phone's screen just fine, no matter how far back the chair took her, mainly because her stomach was now about the size of an overripe grapefruit or a small cantaloupe, but certainly bigger than it was a week ago, and in recent days, seemed to be growing by the minute. Still, despite the stomach and her calves and the fatigue that seemed to hit her this time every day—too close to lunch to justify a snack and too far from dinner to justify a meal—being four months pregnant had its advantages.

Nobody was going to fault her for taking a few minutes for herself in one of the unused salon stations, which was surprisingly private, due to the thin plastic partitions they'd put up because of the pandemic. The milky white plastic sheeting on either side of her was just transparent enough to keep her from feeling claustrophobic, even in a space that was mostly chair, from the footrest just a few bare inches from the mirrored wall that ran the length of the salon, to the headrest, which hovered a few inches over a hair-rinsing bowl that hadn't been used since the place had reopened. Getting your hair done was one thing; Sara would even call it essential, even if the CDC or the president or the governor or whoever seemed to be in charge that particular week disagreed — and the Shiny Locks Salon took every precaution imaginable. The client wore a mask, the stylist wore a mask and a face shield, and everything was kept about as intimate as a really bad first date. But the powers that be had determined: if your head hit that bowl and the warm water was flowing, essential morphed into recreational, and that was a bridge too far.

Of course, Sara wasn't at the Shiny Locks for reasons essential or recreational; she was there for a paycheck. A few inches from her chair, leaning up against the plastic partition, was her broom, which she used to sweep up all those shiny locks, lest they accumulated into dangerous mounds that would threaten to trip up the pair of stylists who catered to the handful of Caledonia's moderate-incomed residents who still cared about their appearance. Which was about four customers a day at best, who came in and out of the shop as if they were pulling off a bank heist: masked, counting the minutes of shared air, using as few words as possible to communicate what they needed. Sara wouldn't have been surprised if most of them left the car running in the parking lot, bottles of hand sanitizer piled up and ready to go.

Even this late into the day, Sara's broom was almost as hair-free as when her husband, Trevor, had dropped her off at work that morning. At the moment, there was only one customer in the salon, two stations down, pretending to read a magazine she'd brought from home—as if everything were normal—as her stylist worked cheap extensions into her hair. Which meant Sarah had plenty of time before she'd need her broom again. Plenty of time for her newest pursuit—something that had been taking up more and more of her downtime, which seemed to far outpace her uptime—marked by the almost neon green glow that was coming from her phone.

Sara couldn't quite remember when she had first downloaded the Robinhood app and opened her trading account, but it was certainly sometime during the past year. Like many others, she assumed, it was that crazy Reddit board that had driven her to the slick online brokerage. Before she'd stumbled onto WallStreetBets, she didn't have any memory of being interested in the stock market. Though she'd taken a few economics courses in college, finance had never really excited her. And like many others, she'd found the WSB board entirely by accident, in the early months of 2020.

At the time, she'd been almost entirely occupied with planning her wedding. Her *dream* wedding, actually, the one that was supposed to have taken place at the end of the year. A couple hundred guests, her entire extended family, a church filled with candles and flowers, her dad walking her down the aisle while everyone stood and smiled and cried and clapped. A reception in the ballroom of a not-quite-luxury-but-really-really-close hotel, with passed hors d'oeuvres and an open bar and a live band. Her dream wedding, which never happened, because Covid, because 2020, *because.*

But at the time, she couldn't have known what was coming, so she'd spent most of her free time digging through wedding sites on the Internet. It was a frog pond hop from pictures of lavish, out-of-her-price-range weddings on Pinterest to postings on Facebook that had eventually led her to a Reddit board dedicated to floral arrangements. Some random evening, as Sara had lurked through a heated discussion about the relative merits of tulips versus lilies, she'd noticed a short thread knocking another, unrelated board. The posters were going on about how perverse and disgusting that other board could be, how it seemed to be dominated by young men who called themselves "retards" and "autists" and "degenerates" and used foul language and dirty memes to make whatever points they were trying to make. Sara had been just bored enough with tulips and lilies to take a look.

When she'd first shifted to the WallStreetBets board, she, too, had been turned off by some of the language. She didn't like the word "retard" and she wasn't sure if what the people were posting—the crazy portfolios showing losses and gains—was real, or just mocked-up bullshit. But she definitely felt the sense of community that was happening at WSB, in a way she hadn't seen on any of the other sites she'd visited. And though the majority of posters might have been men, she was certain that a fair portion of the population was more diverse, more like her, than the critical ladies from the flower board might have realized.

Even so, if Covid hadn't happened, Sara doubted she'd

ever have visited the WSB board again. She'd have been too busy, because 2020 was supposed to have been *her* year. Not just the wedding, but everything. She'd been about to turn thirty, about to get married, her fiancé had just been offered a new job as an IT manager at a small start-up in Denver, Colorado. She and Trevor had made so many plans: They'd found the perfect little town house to rent, with views of the mountains and a short commute to his office. They'd chosen the date for the wedding—October 6—and had even picked out their invitations. Soft white, with flowers at the corners and a little card you filled in with your choice of chicken or fish.

There should have been a third choice—Covid—because every plan they had went right out the window as soon as the pandemic hit. Instead of moving to Colorado, they'd sheltered in place like everyone else. Three months of wiping down groceries, showering after visiting the pharmacy, masks, and even gloves. Sara had watched as friends who had weddings in March and May were forced to cancel, one by one. And with each cancellation, she and Trevor had looked at each other, knowing that October wasn't far enough way—knowing what neither one of them wanted to admit.

They never got to send those invitations. Worse yet, the start-up in Denver lost its financing, and instead of a town house with a view of the mountains, they ended up renting a small two-bedroom in Caledonia, which was closer to Detroit, where they'd both grown up. Trevor had managed to find a new IT job—nothing fancy, working in a back office of a medical device conglomerate—and Sara had taken the job sweeping hair to have something to bring to the table.

The Shiny Locks wasn't anything special, just the sort of chain salon you saw in small towns or strip malls, not dirty, not glamorous—just a place she could make a few bucks with a broom. She'd had bigger plans in terms of work— in Denver, she'd been looking into creative design, something she'd studied a bit in college—but for the moment, it was more important to contribute what she could to the household.

Canceling her dream wedding, opting instead for a small ceremony in the backyard of her parents' house, had been a hard pill to swallow. But the day had been beautiful even so, sunny and clear enough, and her father had indeed walked her down the aisle, even if only a handful of family and close friends had been there to witness the proceedings. And though Sara had mourned the wedding that hadn't happened, shortly afterward, she'd found out the wonderful news that she was expecting. As much as she'd lost in 2020, as much as the pandemic had taken away—she felt she had been given something so much greater. When the baby came, she knew, everything would change. It would be like a fresh start.

But until then, she swept hair, while watching her stomach grow, still pretty much isolated from her friends and family. She had Trevor; but sometimes, even Trevor, as much as she loved him, wasn't enough.

In many ways, the WSB board had filled that void. She knew it was foolish; strangers on some Internet messaging site putting up memes and talking about random stocks in foul language shouldn't have been fulfilling for anyone with half a brain or a quarter of a life—but at the moment, what Sara mostly had was anticipation—of the baby, of things getting better, of one day finding a different job and getting back her social world. Was it so wrong that she spent a few hours a day losing herself in that mindless free-for-all, upvoting risky stock buys and downvoting stupid burns?

Even so, after a few weeks getting more and more addicted to the site, she'd realized that she hadn't mentioned it to anyone else, not even Trevor. She wasn't sure what he would have thought; in their home life, he handled the financial issues—bills, taxes, whatever few investments they'd managed to put together—and they hardly ever talked about money. She couldn't remember them ever really mentioning the stock market—it just wasn't something they discussed.

So she hadn't kept her interest in the WSB board secret on purpose, exactly, but she liked the fact that it was something that was *hers*, something she did that nobody else needed to know about. If Trevor ever did find out, she had no idea what he'd think; but at the very least, she could point to how much she was learning. About Wall Street, finance, stocks.

And it wasn't like she was buying stocks. Not yet, anyway. Reading the board, watching these people she knew only by screen names put huge bets on risky positions, she'd realized that she had some pretty deep feelings about Wall Street, probably dating back to her childhood, growing up in the blue-collared suburbs of Detroit. Her dad had been in the auto business, like everyone else she knew—a shipping manager for a parts supplier—so she'd seen the carnage of 2008 firsthand. Many of her friends' parents had been forced to take buyouts, had eventually lost their houses and moved away. And she'd read the papers like everyone else, the stories about the big Wall Street banks getting bailed out, followed by the auto companies themselves—after all those friends of her family had lost their jobs and homes—and she'd never thought it seemed very fair.

It had made her angry and disappointed, and she'd grown up with a healthy distrust of government. It really did seem like the agencies put in place to protect regular people like her weren't really doing their jobs. It seemed like the only people they were really protecting were the wealthy; the banks, the car companies, the people who were already getting big paychecks and had never had much to worry about in the first place. Even though she was in her twenties, she'd already seen it all: 401(k)s being wiped out, the housing market going to hell, hardworking people getting screwed left and right.

She understood the undercurrent of anger she clearly saw rippling through the WSB posts; though some of the people on the board were clearly just in it to gamble, chasing the rush they got from taking risks—many more were trying to make statements with their money. They were sharing information with each other because they saw themselves aligned against Wall Street, engaged in a sort of tribal class warfare against the wealthy, the advantaged, who had been screwing over regular people like Sara her entire life.

When these same posters pointed her toward Robinhood—an app that gave her the same financial tools the bankers had been using to game the system in their favor for so many years—she'd been intrigued enough to load it onto her phone. She'd even moved a little bit of money over to the app—a few thousand dollars from her wedding budget, which she'd never gotten to spend, along with part of the Covid check—her "stimmy"—they'd received from the government. Twelve hundred dollars—like that was supposed to make any real difference in her life. A couple months' rent, a couple car payments, and then she'd be right back where she'd started. Sweeping hair at a salon while she waited for her baby to be born.

Maybe there really was something else she could do. Maybe those crazy, foul-mouthed, degenerate posters on WallStreetBets were on to something.

Reclining in the chair, running one hand over her grapefruit-cantaloupe belly while she scrolled through the Robinhood app, looking at the charts of stocks she'd read about on WSB—she wondered—would it be so wrong to take a chance?

You couldn't get farther from a Wall Street trading desk than the Shiny Locks Salon in Caledonia, Michigan. But with the information she was getting from the WSB board, married to the powerful tools of the Robinhood app, right under her fingertips—for once, the odds didn't seem so stacked against her, the playing field didn't feel so unfair.

She shook her head, then turned off her phone. She wasn't quite ready to take the next step. All those powerful tools, her new community of gamblers and class warriors— still, she was waiting for something to push her over that edge. Until then, she was content to stay on the sidelines; it was enough that she had this outlet for her frustrations with the world she'd gotten instead of the one she'd expected. At least now she had this secret thing, that was all *hers*.

She slipped the phone back into the pocket of her skirt, then rose from the reclining chair and turned her attention back to her broom.

CHAPTER SEVEN

D ude, everyone thinks I'm crazy, and I think everyone else is crazy...

Keith Gill leaned back in his House Lannister gaming chair as he reached behind his head and pulled the knot on his bandanna tight, feeling the silken material dig into his skin. His entire body was trembling, his chest rising and falling beneath another one of his signature T-shirts — emblazoned with the image of a brindle-colored cat, mid-leap, its claws and jaws open, a feline crazy enough and hungry enough to devour *the whole goddamn world.*

Keith steadied his pulse as he looked across his desk, making sure all the tools of his trade were within reach. His charts, his notepads, his 8-Ball, his Uno cards. He also had something new today: a plate of freshly baked chicken tenders. When he'd been heating them up in the oven, Caroline had thought he was preparing them for his daughter. She'd rolled her eyes when, instead, he'd carried the platter toward the door leading to the basement.

I've dealt in deep value stocks for years but have never endured bearish sentiment this heavy...

Though he doubted he'd be eating any of the "tendies"—the term that had grown popular on the WSB board to symbolize profits made in "stonks," another meme-based WSB expression, a self-deprecating nod toward the general opinion that anyone who followed or gave stock advice via a subreddit that was basically at the basement of the Internet was akin to the kids who used to sit at the back of the class in middle school, eating crayons—during this particular livestream. It hadn't been the best few days, and though Keith remained optimistic—perhaps, as usual, delusionally so—his daughter would probably get her fair shot at the tendies when Caroline brought her home from her afternoon visit to the park.

Keith's laptop was already open and powered up in front of him, but not yet shifted over to the images he would use for the day's livestream, which was set to begin in a few more minutes. Instead, his computer was open to the WSB board. Over the past few weeks he'd become very diligent with his posting to the frenzied stock forum, adding frequent updates of his trading portfolio dovetailing with his YouTube videos and his Twitter. His posts, on the whole, were extremely simple: a screen capture of his trading account, listing all of his positions—including his total account value in dollars, and his daily wins and losses. And in recent months, his posts had been made even simpler by the fact that although he had a few target stocks in his armory, his account now pretty much revolved around a single equity. A single, lone, eggs-in-a-basket asset that he'd gone totally, terrifically, obsessively long into, both through purchases of shares, as well as put options, which allowed him to leverage his bankroll to fairly extreme heights.

I expect the narrative to shift in the second half of the year when investors start looking for ways to play the console refresh and they begin to see what I see...

Keith hadn't set out to fall in love with a single stock. It had started off slowly—more like an infection than an infatuation—almost eighteen months earlier, when the livestream was more an inkling in the back of his head than something that involved cameras and chicken tenders. But now, he had to admit, he was squarely in love, and more than that, in a relationship, as deep and true as any relationship he'd had in real life. And it was a relationship that he'd been diligently sharing through his streams and his posts.

I'll post the update tomorrow as I always do after data readouts. It will be ugly, and everyone will mock me as usual...

His pronouncements had—at first, and for a long time after—been met with mostly ridicule. Which, he also had to admit, had been completely fair. Though he was a grown man wearing a bandanna and a cat T-shirt, not a trader at a desk on Wall Street or even in his faux cubicle at Mass Mutual, he was not, by definition, an amateur. He understood that not everyone would look at the charts that he had compiled, the research he had done, and easily see what appeared so obvious to him. He was educated enough to know that picking stocks was as much magic as it was math. There was no doubt a thin line between genius and delusion, and Keith couldn't be entirely sure which side he fell on. Perhaps the ridicule was on target; perhaps he was so clouded by love that he was seeing something that wasn't entirely there.

But I expect GME to bounce back just as it did after the two previous earnings readouts…

When he had first started buying into GameStop, whose stock exchange ticker was GME, in July 2019, he had felt pretty much alone in his view that the company was being vastly undervalued. Sure, a thirty-five-year-old brick-and-mortar franchise, with over fifty-five hundred stores that specialized in video game consoles, physical game sales and resales, related electronics, and whimsical, countercultural toys like Pickle Rick dolls and *Fortnite* action figures wasn't on anybody's hotlist in a time when everything was going digital and online. The company's sales had dropped more than 13 percent in the first half of 2019 alone, continuing a trend that had been going on for years. This had coincided with a revolving carousel of leadership, with no less than five CEOs named in the past twelve months. Falling sales, vanishing leadership, little to no forward strategy—it was no wonder the stock price had been hovering between $4 and $5 when Keith had first started focusing on the company, and it was less wonder that he was pretty much on his own.

But his initial interest hadn't just been contrarian. He'd applied his strategy of deep research to GameStop and had begun to see things that perhaps others had missed. This wasn't some fly-by-night operation; GameStop was one of the foundational companies in the video game space, a segment of the retail industry that had ballooned to more than $150 billion in 2019 alone—and showed no signs of slowing, as more and more people spent more and more time online. GameStop had failed to take advantage of its built-in customer base and first-mover advantage in gaming to shift beyond its brick-and-mortar weaknesses—but that didn't mean it couldn't pivot. They'd mismanaged the shift on-line like many other businesses before them—Blockbuster, Borders, BlackBerry—and that was just the B's—but that didn't mean there wasn't still time.

Keith also couldn't discount the emotional factor that drew him to GME: like a lot of people from his generation, he *fucking loved GameStop*. Hell, he was sitting in a gaming chair at that very moment; he'd grown up playing video games, and some of his favorite memories had to do with hours spent wandering the aisles at the GameStop in the Westgate Mall in Brockton, finally choosing some video game that he and his brother would devour over a weekend, only to return to the store on Monday to make an exchange. Sure, back then you had no choice but to buy a physical game at a physical store—something that younger kids would look at the same way they'd eye a velociraptor—but the experience was something Keith didn't believe could be entirely duplicated online. And those feelings never really went away.

Maybe Blockbuster made no sense anymore, but that was because the thing Blockbuster had been selling no longer made sense. Games were only getting bigger. Consoles were only getting slicker. The gaming community was only growing stronger.

On top of all this, Keith believed there was an added incentive to making a pick on a stock like GameStop, which everyone else thought was on the verge of collapse. There was so much money aligned on the negative side—so many short positions—that if somehow Keith was right, the ride up could be so much faster than the ride down.

In his job as a financial educator, Keith had spent a fair amount of time breaking down the act—and sometimes art—of short selling, in a way that less savvy customers could understand. When a trader believed a company was in trouble, and its stock was overvalued, they could "borrow" shares, sell them, and then when the stock went down as they'd predicted, rebuy the shares at a lower price, return them to whoever they'd borrowed them from, and pocket the difference. If GameStop was trading at 5, you could borrow 100 shares, sell them for $500; when the stock hit 1, you bought back the 100 shares for $100, returned them, pocketing $400 for yourself. You paid a little fee to the lender for their trouble and came out with a tidy profit.

But what happened if the stock went up instead of down? What happened if GameStop figured out how to capitalize on its millions of nostalgic customers, who spent billions on video games every year? What if the stock went to 10 instead of 1?

What happened was, the short seller was royally screwed. He'd borrowed those 100 shares and sold them at 5. Now the stock was at 10, but he still needed to return his 100 shares. Buying them on the market at 10 meant spending $1000. And what was worse, when he'd borrowed the shares, he'd agreed on a timeline to return them. There was a ticking clock hanging over his head, so he had a choice— buy the shares back at 10 now, losing $500 on the deal—or wait a little longer, hoping the stock went back down before his time limit was up.

And what if he waited, and the stock kept going up? Sooner or later, he had to buy those shares back. Even if the stock went to 15, 20—he was on the hook for those 100 shares. Theoretically, there was no limit to how much he could lose.

Which meant, if somehow GameStop did start to go up, the people who had shorted the company would begin to feel pressure to buy; the more the stock went up, the heavier that pressure became. As the shorts began to cover, buying shares to return them to their lenders, the stock would rise even higher.

In financial parlance, this was something called a "short squeeze." It didn't happen often, but when it did, it could be spectacular. Most famously, in 2008, a surprise takeover attempt of the German automaker Volkswagen by rival Porsche drove Volkswagen's stock price up by a factor of 5—briefly making it the most valuable company in the world—in two quick days of trading, as short selling funds struggled to cover their positions. Similarly, a battle between two hedge fund titans—Bill Ackman, of Pershing Square Capital Management, and Carl Icahn— led to a squeeze involving supplement maker—and alleged pyramid marketer—Herbalife, which cost Ackman a re- ported $1 billion. And perhaps the first widely reported short squeeze dated back a century, to 1923, when grocery magnate Clarence Saunders successfully decimated short sellers who had targeted his nascent chain of Piggly Wiggly grocery stores.

Because so many people were betting against GameStop— and brick-and-mortar retail in general—the overall short position was enormous, almost comically so. At certain points over the past six months, it had bounced between 50 and even 100 percent of the overall float, meaning nearly all the shares of GameStop in existence had been borrowed and sold by short sellers, all of whom had an obligation to rebuy those shares at some point in the future.

So, what if Keith was right, and the stock went up instead of down? It would be like watching investors trying to get out of a burning building, through a single, narrow door. The stock would rocket.

As a financial educator, Keith knew that short selling could be one of the riskiest plays on the market. You really needed to be certain a stock was going down, because your upside was limited, but your losses could, theoretically, be infinite. The fact that so many competent investors were short selling GameStop could mean the stock really was a dog; but it also meant the stock was loaded with rocket fuel, and it wouldn't take much to ignite and send it right to the moon.

So, Keith had bought in. A little at first—but buying stocks, especially in the age of Robinhood, was addictive. A few thousand dollars rapidly became a total stake of $53,000, some in straight equity, some via call options. Keith was sophisticated enough to understand the inherent risk of options; buying options wasn't as dangerous as short selling, because your potential for loss was capped, because you could always let the options expire. You paid a fee for the right to buy a certain number of shares of a stock at a certain price by a certain date. Sold in 100-share blocks, the fee was based on demand, which related to where people thought the stock price was going. Because the fee you paid for those 100-share blocks was a fraction of the pegged price, you could leverage yourself into a very large position with a relatively small amount of money. If the price went up, you could make a lot; if it went down, your options were worthless, but you only lost what you initially invested.

A full 80 percent of the options bought by retail traders like him expired worthless; but when you only had a little to work with, there was no better way to shoot for the moon. Fifty-three thousand dollars was a lot, considering he had a two-year-old, a house, a wife. It was as much money as his dad earned in a year when he was younger. But Keith was that sure, even when the stock was hovering around $5 a share, that he had found value that others had missed.

When he'd first posted on WallStreetBets about Game-Stop, the responses had varied between amusement and outright hostility. That hadn't changed until August 2019, when Keith had woken up on a Thursday to find the stock spiking as much as 20 percent; as it turned out, Michael Burry, the famous investor and hedge fund manager who had predicted the real estate crash of 2008 and had been featured in the Michael Lewis and Adam McKay movie *The Big Short*, had written a letter to the GameStop board revealing that his Scion Asset Management had bought 3 percent of the company's available stock—2,750,000 shares—and believed that GameStop was in much better shape than anyone realized. In an interview with *Barron's*, Burry had further pointed out that Sony and Microsoft were going to be launching consoles—and neither company had yet abandoned the physical disc drive, even if a significant portion of gamers had begun their games as digital downloads—which would draw more customers to GameStop—and that GameStop's current situation "looks worse than it really is."

Burry's buy didn't just bolster the stock price; it

galvanized a portion of the community on the WSB board—or at least warmed them to the idea that Keith might not be entirely crazy. The WSB board had a certain affinity for Burry; Burry self-identified as someone with Asperger syndrome, on the autism spectrum, and his quirky character in the movie, portrayed by Christian Bale, was extremely relatable to the subversives who often referred to themselves as "autists" in their comments. In some ways, the self-deprecation was a defense mechanism, and a way of marking the community as an antithesis to the mainstream: WSB wasn't populated by Masters of the Universe; it was populated by "retards" whose wives all had boyfriends.

After Burry's letter and the resulting market effect, Keith's star had begun to rise on the WSB board. That afternoon, affixed to his regular post, he wrote:

Hey Burry thanks a lot for jacking up my cost basis.

When a poster calling himself Techmonk123 responded:

Holy shit bro, what made you drop 53k on GameStop?

Keith had fired back:

The fact that it's worth quite a bit more than $8/sh and there are numerous catalysts that could trigger a reversion to fair value over the next 18 mo.

He'd more than doubled his initial investment—and was sitting on a balance of over $113,000, but still the skeptics had far outnumbered the converted. His Roaring Kitty videos still had fewer than five hundred viewers.

Over $100,000—Keith knew that he could have used that money to make changes in his life. Perhaps buy a house instead of rent, go on a trip somewhere. But with Burry in, he wasn't about to sell.

You're letting hope and dreams take over instead of listening to the market, another skeptic had posted. And at the time, Keith could only respond with honesty:

Why are you suggesting my thesis is grounded in "hope and dreams" and not legitimate analysis?

As the months had passed, Keith hadn't altered his opinions, or wavered in his beliefs. Even before GameStop had been forced by the pandemic to close all of its US stores, and even before they had released their abysmal 2019 holiday sales figures—Keith had dutifully continued posting his statements, filled with so much more blood red than green, as he gave back nearly every penny he'd gained.

When a commenter calling himself "brutalpancake" challenged him on his determination:

Man there's deep value—and then there's a rotting carcass. To me this thing started to stink a while ago. Keith had responded with what became a bit of a personal motto:

Yea there's deep value, then there's deep fucking value.

Sure, a part of Keith knew that what he was doing was crazy. He was a grown man sitting in his basement with a bandanna tied around his head, wearing a cat T-shirt, contemplating a tray filled with chicken tenders. A grown man with a YouTube channel under the name "Roaring Kitty," posting on a subreddit under the handle DeepFuckingValue.

That rational part of him knew: love could be dangerous. The belief that powered you forward could become the thing that killed you.

But even if that was true—hell, he wouldn't be the first grown man destroyed by love.

CHAPTER EIGHT

S ounds like a soft drink."

The lines around Jeremy's dad's eyes crisscrossed into a dramatic squint, adding years to his still mostly youthful appearance, as he sized up the water trap just a dozen yards ahead of them down the fairway. Even with his rapidly receding hairline and the sprinkle of gray that ran through the waves of what was left of his hair on either side, Andrew Poe didn't look like a man pushing fifty. But the more he talked, the less likely anyone would confuse him with anything other than a middle-aged dad.

"Or maybe a Brazilian television show. You sure you're saying it right?"

"Just take your swing already. We both know it's going in the lake."

His dad finally turned his attention to the ball in front of his boots, which rested on a patch of frost-covered grass. He gripped the golf club with both hands, then awkwardly leaned forward to get the head of the thing close enough to the ground. The club was much too short for his nearly six-foot frame, and there was a slight bend in the metal right below the grip. It had been like that when they'd picked up the club at a neighbor's garage sale during Jeremy's last visit to his parents' home, around Thanksgiving. The neighbor had tried to sell them an entire set, along with a scuffed bag—but Jeremy's dad had figured the one club and a handful of balls were enough for a start. Neither one of them actually knew how to play golf, after all.

"YOLO," his dad said, squaring up for his swing. "It does sound kind of cool, though."

He raised the club over his shoulder, even more awkward now, clearly the motion of a man who'd never taken a golf lesson in his life. Neither of them had any business wandering around the sixth hole of a course like the Sugar Mountain County Golf Club, even if it was a public course at the tail end of December, and the ground was covered in frost—there was even snow piled up by the hole, which was on the other side of the partially frozen lake, though it may as well have been on the other side of North Carolina, for all the likelihood that they would get the ball anywhere near it.

Still, it was nice being outside with his dad, and it was especially nice because it was, after all, Christmas break. It didn't usually snow this early in the season; maybe that, too, had to do with the pandemic. Maybe because nobody was going anywhere, global warming had just plain stopped, and Sugar Mountain, North Carolina, was on its way toward another ice age.

The long drive from Durham to his parents' house in the resort town up in the Blue Ridge Mountains had been both fun and annoying; the traffic had been sparse, the scenery beautiful along the three-hour straight shot down US 421, but Jeremy had been forced to listen to his brother rattle on about his dorm life for much of the trip. Even with all the restrictions, it was clear Casper was having a better time at school than Jeremy, which was why Jeremy had made sure they were both wearing masks for most of the trip, and he'd both test and quarantine when he got back on campus. He owed that much to his bubble, after all.

But outside, on the golf course with his dad, Jeremy could feel almost normal. His mask was off, because the breeze was blowing and his dad kept a healthy distance, and besides, there was nobody else around. Which was probably a good thing, because they weren't exactly wearing golf attire. Jeans, sweatshirts, jackets, and Jeremy was in sneakers while his dad had on weird, fur-lined boots he'd bought in the shop at an American Indian casino west of Asheville. Worse yet, they had only the one club between them, which his dad suddenly brought down in a mighty swing—connecting with the ball and sending it skittering forward at a terrifying angle, more a line drive than a gravity-defying arc. The ball made it halfway across the lake before descending to the icy surface. Two skips and a jump, and then it plunked deep into the water.

"You can't teach that," his dad said.

Despite the ugly shot, Jeremy knew that his dad was more of an athlete than either he or his brother, who got their elongated physiques from their mom. Andrew Poe had played multiple sports in high school before settling on soccer in college. He'd remained mostly in shape as he'd aged, though he was a little rounder around the middle than Jeremy remembered from his childhood. But seeing some extra weight on his dad didn't bother Jeremy—quite the contrary. Most of the time, Jeremy could forget that his dad still saw the oncologist every couple of months for routine checkups, but he doubted he'd ever stop worrying about any changes he noticed in his dad's health or demeanor.

"You must have practiced while I was at school," Jeremy said as he took the club from his dad. Then Jeremy reached into the pocket of his jacket, retrieved another golf ball, and dropped it in front of his shoes.

"Of course," his dad responded. "Been out here every morning with your mom since we moved in. So this YOLO. It's, like, a motto?"

Jeremy tapped the ground with the head of the club, checking its weight.

"It's more of a financial strategy. You do the research. You dig into the fundamentals. You weigh the risks and the opportunity for profit. And then you bet it all."

Jeremy lifted the club over his shoulder, took aim, and swung with all his strength. The head of the club missed the ball by a good half-foot, and Jeremy nearly toppled over from the inertia. When he finally steadied himself, he was smiling.

He had to admit, it did sound kind of ridiculous. YOLO ("You Only Live Once") seemed the sort of tautism you read in a self-help book, urging you not to sweat the little things, and maybe book that trip to Ibiza or splurge on that new leather coat. But as an approach to investing, it bordered on the profane. And yet the more time Jeremy spent on the WSB board, the more he'd become convinced that for regular young people like himself, caught up in this irregular moment in time, facing a historically uneven playing field, there was a perverse logic behind shooting for the moon.

Jeremy wasn't surprised that a large faction of the WSB board had, over the past few weeks, been galvanizing around the trading philosophy—specifically, as represented by one of the fastest-growing stars on the site, a poster calling himself DeepFuckingValue. Since discovering DFV's GameStop posts, Jeremy had spent many hours watching the guy's livestreams on YouTube, which he put up under the name "Roaring Kitty," and Jeremy had to admit the guy was really charismatic. DFV was smart, open with his research, and explained the logic behind his trades in easy-to-understand terms. He didn't seem to be trying to snow anyone, and he didn't seem to have any ulterior motives. He just really loved GameStop and had decided to take a YOLO position on it, putting down as much money as he could on a bet that the stock was going to the moon.

And shockingly, that bet hadn't evaporated like 90 percent of the YOLO trades Jeremy had followed on the site. In fact, it had gone staggeringly well for DFV. Although the stock's fortunes had changed slightly for the better after Michael Burry had announced his interest in the company in the summer of 2019, things had really begun to roll just a couple months ago, when in late August an SEC filing had reached the attention of DFV and his followers on YouTube and the Reddit board. On August 28, an entrepreneur and near-billionaire named Ryan Cohen had filed with the SEC that he had quietly acquired 10 percent of the company's float—9 million shares—at around $8 a share. Cohen had put $76 million behind his belief that GameStop could turn things around; but unlike DFV, who was basically a guy on the Internet who liked cats, Cohen was an e-commerce genius, who ten years ago had founded an online pet food company called Chewy with $15 million in capital—and had then grown it into a quarter-billion-dollar-revenue business that he'd sold to PetSmart for $3.35 billion. When Chewy had gone public in 2019, its value had exploded to over $43 billion.

Cohen's investment in GameStop had been a major catalyst for the stock, driving it up over the next couple of months by a factor of 5. And that rise had turned DFV from just another voice on WSB to one of its legends.

Jeremy had nearly memorized the video the man had posted, just two days earlier, on Christmas, December 25—marking the crazy run he'd already been on with the stock. In that video, posted under his Roaring Kitty account and titled "LESSSSSSSSSSSSGOOOOOO," DFV had looked uncharacteristically overwhelmed. He was still in his signature red bandanna, but instead of a cat T-shirt, he'd had on a black tee with the slogan "GAME OVER" in video game font, a nod back to nearly every video game from the eighties and nineties, which ended with those wonderful, unavoidable words.

"Hey, what's up, everybody, cheers!" DFV had started the video, and then he'd gotten right to the point: his $53,000 investment in GameStop had turned into over *$1 million* in profits. DFV had appeared as flabbergasted by the turn of events as anyone. He was just a regular guy: "I certainly do not drive a Lambo, we rent this house that you see, it's been a wild ride for us as a family, and it has been so much fun to have experienced that with you over the past couple of months." To Jeremy, it was such an incredible thing to witness—and it didn't seem to be the result of some lucky gamble that had paid off. It really seemed like it was the culmination of a *strategy*.

"See," Jeremy said as he moved back into a reasonable facsimile of a golf stance, "the thinking is, if you're a big Wall Street bank, or some rich guy in a mansion, you can afford to diversify your portfolio. Take away the risk, aim for regular, solid returns. But when you're some normal shmo with a mortgage or school loans or car payments due—"

"This Roaring Kitty."

"Right. When you're someone like, well, us—diversifying is just a way to tread water. Earning a little here and there doesn't get you anywhere. When you finally sell your positions, you still have the same problems you had before. You still have the same life, with the same bills to pay—"

"Bills? Who pays bills?"

Jeremy laughed. He knew he was privileged—his dad still sent him checks every month to cover his living expenses and tuition. Before Covid, he had worked part time doing data science for a professor to help cover his student loans, but now he was mostly on the parental dole. He knew there were a lot of people on the WSB board who were a lot worse off than he was. The pandemic had hit the community hard, and many were out of work. Which made it more understandable, to Jeremy, that they were willing to try to use whatever little money they had to change things, and not just incrementally—but monumentally.

"You know what I mean," Jeremy said. "So instead of listening to the sorts of financial advisors who write columns in *USA Today* or talk down to you on CNBC, you do your own research, then dig as deep as you can and go big. You go all the way big."

Jeremy swung the club again, this time making contact with the ball. Instead of going forward toward the lake, the ball shot off to the right, slapping right into a low snowbank. Jeremy shook his head, reached into his pocket for another ball.

"I get it," his dad said. "Diversifying is for boomers. Not for the kids in the back of the class. With the crayons."

Jeremy raised his eyebrows. Obviously, his dad had been paying attention to at least some of the e-mails and phone conversations he'd had with Jeremy over the past week before Christmas break; maybe he'd even spent time on the WSB board himself, checking out DFV's posts—each one titled "GME YOLO Update" and the responses, maybe even some of the ridiculous memes. Jeremy was sure much of it had gone over his dad's head—or more accurately, beneath his sensibilities. Repurposed scenes from *Planet of the Apes* or *Star Wars*, let alone videos of people drinking pee because they lost a bet on a stock, were not going to convince his dad that the board was a place to go for sound financial advice. But as Jeremy had tried to explain, the board functioned in the language of its peer group. If Jeremy had been living through his senior year in a regular era, he'd be talking to his friends in bars, at dorm parties, maybe even at frat houses. Instead, he was socializing over the Internet, in a frat called WallStreetBets.

YOLO was something that made perfect sense in that environment. And Jeremy had come to believe YOLO investing in GameStop made even more sense. Not just because of what Roaring Kitty was telling him about the stock's potential; Jeremy could see that the company's fundamentals had issues, and there was little reason to believe their management had the fortitude to right the ship. And heck, Jeremy knew how out of date the current incarnation of GameStop felt to anyone who'd visited one of the company's many franchises in recent years. Walking into a GameStop was a little like stumbling into a flash mob equivalent of a garage sale; items strewn about with no sense of order, used video games piled up next to plush toys and random entertainment-related merchandise. Wandering that maze of shelves was disjointing and sometimes terrifying; a line of fuzzy pink stuffed animals might suddenly end with some horrifying rodent-creature holding a blood-soaked chain saw.

And if, somehow, you did find what you were looking for, checking out was always an adventure. There was always a line, and it was always moving like an ice floe; the store clerks often seemed as needy, lonely, and conversation-starved as the franchise's stereotypical customer.

But even so, Jeremy believed GameStop could change. He believed Ryan Cohen was really going to help the company—and the WSB community was beginning to rally around GME. More and more of them were following DFV into the trade, and Jeremy understood there was power in that. And it was something he wanted his dad to understand, too.

Jeremy knew—his dad had as much YOLO in him as anyone on the WSB board. Jeremy could still vividly remember the day when his father had come home early from his job at a mid-level law firm outside Raleigh, where Jeremy had lived until the age of seven, and announced to the family that he wanted to drop everything and buy a boat. Right in his prime earning years—as his boss at the law firm had whined—he'd packed up the family and taken them to sea, carting them all down to Florida and then the Bahamas, to a life spent traipsing between islands while homeschooling, splayed out on the canvas of a catamaran.

Seven, eight, nine years old, Jeremy had lived this crazy, idyllic life, wondering if his dad had gone insane, or had made the best decision anyone could make. Until at ten, his dad had finally sat him down, next to his brother, and told him the secret he'd been carrying since they'd left North Carolina.

Cancer, in his kidneys, and aggressive.

That night, Jeremy had gone online and delved into what his father had told him; even then, Jeremy had been good on the computer, stealing as much Wi-Fi as he could whenever the catamaran was within shouting distance of a port or a bigger, more technically equipped boat. Even a ten-year-old's depth of research told him that his dad's odds weren't good. To make matters worse, the timing of his dad's cancer diagnosis had coincided with the financial collapse of 2008; the market was plummeting. So his dad hadn't just quit his job, which he'd potentially have lost anyway, but he'd also contemplated the possibility that he'd die, leaving two young children for his wife to support— and he'd sold all of his stocks and his house, and moved the family to the boat.

Thankfully, Jeremy had gotten lucky; his father had beaten the odds and, through surgery and treatment, had managed to survive his cancer and rebuild his health and much of his bank account; he'd gone back to a position in the legal field, and recently bought the home in Sugar Mountain. But deep lessons had been learned along the way, about how quickly things could change, how unfair life could be, and how taking a chance and doing something crazy was often the right play to make.

"So how much are you thinking?" Jeremy's dad asked, and Jeremy could hear the change in his voice. Despite the memes, perhaps something on the board had gotten through to him? Michael Burry, the growing short interest, DFV's unfailing optimism? Or maybe he believed it was finally time to let Jeremy pilot the boat.

"I've got around six thousand dollars in my school account," Jeremy responded.

"That's for textbooks. And food."

"Both are overrated."

"Jeremy."

Jeremy swung the club again, hitting his second ball square in the center. The ball went up in a reasonable arc, then plunked straight down into the lake. His dad clapped him on the back, and the contact felt good, because at the tail end of 2020, just about any contact felt good.

"Maybe I'll buy some, too," his dad said. "YOLO, right?"

And then he grinned, reaching for the club.

CHAPTER NINE

The adrenaline rush took Kim by surprise as she raised her finger over the pill-shaped, orange digital button on the bottom right corner of her phone's screen. She hesitated for a moment, letting the feeling wash through her. She'd been bone tired from another long shift just a few minutes ago, when she'd first sat down at the table in her small, functional kitchenette, pushing aside a stack of her older son Brian's schoolbooks and nearly upending one of her younger son—Kyle's—latest Lego constructions, something resembling either a submarine or a megalodon, depending on whether the thing sticking out of the top was a fin or a periscope. Now, the exhaustion had completely left her body. She was about to do something out of character, exciting, and maybe a little crazy.

And boy, did that feel good.

She glanced beyond the table, across her compact living room to the hallway that led to her sons' bedrooms on the other side of the apartment. It was a little after 9 p.m., one of those miraculous instances when the house was quiet. Kim didn't believe for a moment her kids were actually asleep.

No doubt Brian had his iPad out from its hiding place under his mattress—why did fifteen-year-old boys think moms didn't know about mattresses?—and Kyle was probably under his covers with a flashlight, working on building something with Popsicle sticks, which were his current obsession, or maybe tinkering with the Lego Death Star she'd gotten him for his last birthday from some website in China for a tenth of its American price. Her ex had given her a hard time about the Death Star, saying it was setting the poor kid up for "unattainable expectations" or some other such nonsense, but Kim had let the comment slide without putting up much of a fight. Things were good with her ex; actually, for once, things were pretty good with both of her kids' fathers, which happened about as frequently as a full lunar eclipse—so she hadn't wanted to do anything to rock the boat. Her life could be hard enough without having to deal with bickering old flames.

Besides, she wasn't doing poorly, all things considered. Her apartment had three bedrooms, a new dishwasher, and windows that overlooked a quiet courtyard, and the complex surrounding her was mostly new construction, which meant things weren't falling apart yet. And her neighbors were nice, mostly professionals who respected her because she came home in scrubs and her kids didn't light fires in the hallways.

Actually, they were really good kids, who had made the best of what could have seemed a pretty dysfunctional situation. Brian split his time between her home and his dad's, and they all did their best to get along. She and Brian's dad hadn't been to court—because technically, they'd never been married in the first place.

They'd met in college—Penn State—as freshmen; Kim had been a fencer and Brian's dad a member of the lacrosse team. They'd gotten close extremely fast and, by the end of freshman year, had been spending every night together in each other's dorms.

It was the day after Kim had gotten home for winter break her sophomore year when she'd realized something was off and took her first pregnancy test. Having a baby at nineteen had not been part of either of their plans, but somehow Kim had still managed to finish out her sophomore year at Penn State, before moving back in with her parents to have the baby. When she'd started up again at California State University in the fall, things between her and her ex had gone sour. She had realized, then, that life was something she was going to have to get good at on her own.

Six years later, she was caring for a precocious kid while just starting out as an RN, when baby daddy number two came into the picture. It had started as a Facebook friend request from one of her ex's college lacrosse teammates, who, it turned out, had always had a crush on her. A few innocent messages had turned into a relationship, which had then led to her taking a spontaneous trip to Massachusetts to pack up all his stuff, including two dogs and two chinchillas, and driving back across the country to California. A few months later, they'd had a backyard wedding, with her son as the ring bearer. Kyle had come along a short time later, and then things had fizzled with dad number two, leading to divorce, many court dates, more than a few missed child support checks, and her ending up a walking cliché, single mother of two carrying a whole lot of debt and her fair share of broken dreams.

But she was on much better terms with dad number two now that Kyle was a bit older, and her nursing career had taken care of much of her debt. Child support wasn't something she could count on, but both her kids were well adapted and happy. She had her hands full with the two of them, and her house was usually a wreck. Brian was often in his room, but Kyle had a way of taking over whatever space he was in with his projects. Popsicle sticks could swallow a bedroom, and a package of balloons could somehow take over her living room; but once she'd accepted that her house was a battle that she'd always be on the losing end of, things had gotten better.

Still, the moments of downtime, when she was alone after the kids had turned out their lights, felt like little miracles—and this particular moment seemed even more blessed, because she'd been waiting for it since she'd clocked in at work.

She knew she could be an obsessive person and had a tendency to get carried away with things—and she'd had plenty of hobbies before. Fencing in high school and college, self-improvement, which had led her on a yearlong dip into the teachings of Tony Robbins in her twenties—she'd even gone to a few of his weekend retreats, learning how to identify her needs, focus her energy, make decisions that led to real change—and of course, Trump. She'd also spent months delving into her own ancestry, spurred on by her best friend Angie, who had coaxed her to apply to a charitable organization called the Daughters of the American Revolution, whose main membership requirement was that you found a direct relative who had been a verified American patriot. Enough targeted digging, and Kim had found a bunch of relatives who qualified, including a great-great-great-uncle who'd carried a musket, though she wasn't certain he'd ever pointed it at anyone.

When she set her mind to something, she knew how to go deep.

But what was going on between her and the WallStreetBets board was something on an entirely different level. What had started as a fun way to spend her free time at work and home, browsing messages and applauding good stock buys and making fun of atrocious losses, had morphed into an active pastime. Not only was she posting on the board—mostly questions about financial tactics and particular stocks—she had even stuck her toe into the pond, using her Robinhood account to buy a handful of stocks after reading posts that were particularly persuasive. Nothing serious—because Robinhood had no account requirements, she'd been able to put in a few hundred dollars and throw it at tickers. And even though she'd lost most of it, the thrill had been undeniable.

Now, she was ready to go even further, because over the past few weeks she'd watched, like everyone else on the WSB board, something that felt unique and significant.

She didn't know a lot about GameStop. Her older son loved it, of course, because he spent most of his time playing video games. And though he downloaded most everything directly from the Net, there was still something fun about walking around a store dedicated to the type of people who knew the difference between *Fortnite* and *Roblox*. But Kim didn't care so much about GameStop, the company—because she was finding herself completely caught up in GME, the meme "stonk."

It had started with DFV's posts and livestreams. She'd gone back through them as if she'd been researching her own ancestry, looking for a patriot—looking for whatever it was that had made Roaring Kitty fall so in love with the stock that he was willing to put what had to be most of his money into one big bet. She'd listened as he'd told her about Michael Burry and Ryan Cohen, and their support of the company. She'd taken notes as he'd talked about the short interest, and what it might mean for a stock to have nearly all of its shares shorted. And she'd watched, in awe, as he'd turned that $53,000 bet into a $1 million fortune.

And the thing about the way the WSB board worked, it wasn't some high-and-mighty figure on TV talking to an audience, or some "expert" throwing out terms she'd never hope to understand. DFV was just another ape, another retard, talking about this crazy thing he believed in.

Kim loved every minute of it, and she wanted *in*. She knew that part of what was driving her was FOMO—a fear of missing out on something that had already turned this regular dude with a mullet and a cat fixation into a millionaire. And she knew that she was less swayed by the long, drawn-out due diligence posts that often accompanied DFV's comments than the cult of personality that had developed around him and his YOLO attitude.

Once she'd decided to get off the sidelines, it had just become a matter of picking her moment—and the amount she could bet, if not responsibly, at least without risking her family's station. Overall, she was a pretty frugal person: She still drove her 2006 Honda with over 230,000 miles on it. She bought all her and her children's clothes at thrift stores. She used coupons religiously, and only shopped during sales. She also had a 403(b) through her work, which had a nice little nest egg built up for her retirement. It was all put into some safe Vanguard ETFs and, despite the corona dip, was still holding its own.

Since she'd already lost about $400 on random stocks she'd read about on the WSB board, she had to be careful—but she'd cautiously moved $5000 into a trading account. It was a large amount—but it was a figure she'd chosen for two reasons. She felt comfortable that they could survive losing the entire thing; and if DFV was right, and GameStop could—at best, she figured—double from where it was sitting at around $16 a share, she would make enough to pay for Brian's braces.

Her plan was to start with 100 shares. Compared to some of the posts she'd read on the board, it was a pittance; but for her, it was enormous, and she felt the moment in every cell as she finally brought her finger down on that Buy button.

Although it was after market hours, the Robinhood account seemed as thrilled as she felt. The phone vibrated in her hand, and though she didn't get confetti—she'd already enjoyed that spectacle when she'd bought the crap tickers weeks earlier—she did get a nice pulse of dopamine in her veins. Tomorrow morning, when the market opened, Robinhood would fire its arrows toward Citadel or Two Sigma or Susquehanna, and Kim would be well on her way.

CHAPTER TEN

No matter how much they tried to dress up the examination room—the jungle of potted plants by the door, the glossy posters of sun-bleached Greek Islands on the walls, the soft Muzak fluttering out of speakers hidden behind mountains of medical equipment, even the overpowered ventilation system that failed to mask the antiseptic bouquet characteristic of any remotely medical location—Sara couldn't shake the anxiety that always seemed to hit her in places like this.

And even though her husband was waiting just outside in their car—owing to Michigan's tough Covid precautions, and the nurse, in her light blue scrubs and mask and face shield was presumably smiling and warm and talking like this was the most routine thing in the world—Sara couldn't help but feel intensely vulnerable. Lying back on a table surrounded by machines and a masked stranger was surreal enough; she was doing so with her shirt pulled up to reveal her bare stomach, which was now clearly way past grapefruit and deep into cantaloupe—even trending upward along the Cucumis scale, heading right toward goddamn *watermelon*.

The nurse was quickly joined by an ob-gyn, who swept into the room, gowned and gloved, as if he were about to conduct an orchestra. The man's jowls were hidden beneath his mask, but his eyes lit up behind his glasses, and that, alone, made Sara feel a bit more at ease. Looking at him, imagining the smile that she couldn't see, she knew she was being foolish; this really was routine, and she was young and healthy and pregnant.

And getting more pregnant by the day.

The doctor gave her shoulder a friendly squeeze, then moved to the machine next to her bed, checking the screen. The machine was turned away from her, but she could see the greenish glow reflected off one of the glossy posters on the wall, flickering pixels surfing the waves that frolicked off the Amalfi Coast.

The doctor said something to the nurse, and the woman approached the table, then gently helped Sara lift her shirt a little farther up her stomach.

"This is gonna feel a little cold," the nurse said as she squirted some sort of clear gel onto Sara's stomach from a white tube.

Then she moved aside, and the doctor approached, holding a small, pokey-shaped device attached to a long cord. He placed the device right against the skin of her stomach, harder than Sara had expected. She flinched against the pressure; then the doctor moved the device around, pressing inward here and there. He was looking back at the machine, so Sara did, too; she still couldn't see the screen fully, but it had angled a bit more toward her with the doctor's motion. She could now make out fuzzy lines, and she squinted, trying to make sense of them. The doctor kept moving the device, obviously searching for something. He was also clicking buttons on a keyboard attached below the screen. Sara held her breath, wanting him to find what he was looking for, but also fighting the sudden urge the pressure was bringing on to laugh and pee at the same time. Laughing would be fine, she figured, but she really hoped she didn't pee on the table. That would have been embarrassing.

The doctor stopped moving, and the way his eyes crinkled, she could imagine his smile widening. He nodded to the nurse, who hit another key on the keyboard—and then a noise filled the room. A thump, thump, thump.

"Is that?" Sara asked.

The doctor nodded, then pointed to a spot on the screen. Sara could see it now—a little sac of motion, the beating heart. And then, nearby, a head, or what she thought might be a head, and a little hand, reaching out.

"It's beautiful," she said.

She couldn't believe she was looking at her baby. Boy or girl—she didn't know yet—and she wasn't sure she wanted to know. But she was looking at her child. In a matter of months, that child was going to spring out into the world. Would it still be a place of masks and quarantines? Sara only knew that, for her, that little heartbeat meant that nothing was going to be the same, and for that, she was immensely thankful.

She wished Trevor could have been there, next to her, squeezing her hand. She thought of him alone in the car; probably worried, but probably also handling work calls, one after another; for days now, she'd been coming home from the salon to an empty house, making dinner for herself and leaving his half in Tupperware containers in the fridge.

She understood—and the tiny creature on the screen across the exam room made her understand even more. Although 2020 was coming to a rapid close, things hadn't gotten any easier for them yet.

Her thoughts were interrupted when the doctor hit another key on the keyboard, freezing the screen.

"You want a souvenir?" he asked.

When she nodded, he receded toward an adjoining room, where a different machine would print out the photo. The nurse handed Sara a wad of tissues for her stomach, then headed after the doctor, leaving Sara alone to the job.

Sara did what she could with the mess on her skin, then pulled her shirt back over her bump. Still by herself in the room, she wasn't sure if she should get up from the table; instead, she decided to wait—and retrieved her phone from her purse, which was on a chair close enough to reach. She was about to text her husband and then her mother, tell them about that little peanut and the heartbeat and the hand—but instead, found herself in a familiar place, one that should have felt completely wrong in an examination room, lying on a table, with the frozen image of her baby on a screen nearby—but somehow, didn't.

In the past few weeks, the WSB board had become a second home, as much a part of her life as Facebook or Instagram had ever been. It made her smile, and lately, it had also made her think. Because something new was happening—something dramatic, and something wild.

She'd read all of DFV's posts—how could she not have, they had risen to the top of the board and were drawing a huge following now. She'd also watched some of his livestreams—though who had time for five-hour-long free-for-alls about GameStop, no matter how charismatic the guy was? And she'd scrolled through many of the comments about what he'd been saying, both on YouTube and WallStreetBets.

It was obvious, a lot of people were buying in, and the stock had risen to close to $20 a share. Which, she gathered, had been DFV's original price target when he'd first started posting about the company being undervalued. But Sara didn't believe that stock rise had much to do with the bits of news he'd gone on about, the interest of that strange guy from *The Big Short*, or even the meme-friendly pet food entrepreneur.

She believed something deeper was happening.

Alone in the examining room, waiting for the doctor to return, she scrolled through WallStreetBets to a post she had bookmarked, which she'd first found when she'd been reading backward through different comment streams to try and understand more about what was going on. That was one of the great things about Reddit—and the Internet in general. As the saying went, it wasn't written in pencil, but pen, and once something was dropped into that ether, no matter how innocuous, it could grow to have a life of its own.

Of course, the meme-like video that had been posted on October 27 to the WSB board by someone calling himself Stonksflyingup had been anything but innocuous. The post, "GME Squeeze and the Demise of Melvin Capital," was a video lifted from the television miniseries *Chernobyl*, about the meltdown of a nuclear reactor in Russia that had caused an international catastrophe. Stonksflyingup had added subtitles of his own to the video, equating what he believed was going to happen to something called *Melvin Capital*—apparently, a large Wall Street hedge fund with a massive short position in GameStop—with the meltdown at Chernobyl; how the battle between the GameStop longs and the Wall Street shorts would end with Melvin exploding in a fiery, nuclear blast.

The video had turned into an immediate sensation on the board. Reading back through hundreds of comments, Sara could see—Melvin Capital hadn't been picked at random for the video. The seething anger toward Wall Street that so many people on the board had enunciated in so many different memes, comments, diatribes, now had a focus, a *face*.

From what Sara had read, Melvin Capital had come to the attention of the board at the beginning of the fall after it had filed SEC paperwork called a Form 13F, in which it had disclosed a short option position in GameStop, tucked in with a number of other seemingly routine trades. But since the form was public, and members of the WSB board had been motivated—and bored—enough to sift through every SEC filing they could find, looking for anything having to do with GameStop—with the 13F, Melvin had unwittingly made itself into a perfect scapegoat. To the WSB board, Melvin suddenly represented everything about Wall Street they hated. A staid, respected, multibillion-dollar firm, run by men in suits, looking to profit on the failings of a beloved, if mismanaged, company.

Sara could see it in the posts that followed the video: Something had seriously changed. People were no longer just buying GameStop to try and make money. In fact, many of the comments said quite the opposite—people were willing, even happy, to *lose* every penny they put into GME, to try and stick it to Melvin, to strike a blow against what they represented.

GME wasn't just some stock anymore. It was a token, a meme, and it symbolized something dark and striking and of the moment.

Lying there, still feeling vulnerable on that examination table, her new baby growing inside her—Sara understood that moment because she was living it. She felt it in her soul.

The bubbling, unsettled anger and confusion and god-damn boredom of millions upon millions stuck at home, losing their jobs and watching their bank accounts dwindle, completely without a voice—and then fuck, some hedge fund shorts GameStop and, well, *of course they do*. Because maybe GameStop doesn't make much sense anymore when we're all watching the apocalypse unfold, ordering our groceries from Instacart and our dinner from DoorDash and our toilet paper from Amazon. And yeah, sure, Game-Stop was dying before any of this, like every other brick-and-mortar business—nobody had cried over Blockbuster or Borders or Tower Records. So the hedgies like Melvin are going to make that bet and get even richer, and take yet another thing away from us. But—the battle cry went—maybe this time it didn't have to happen that way. Maybe for once we could do something, stop something, have a voice, make a difference.

GME wasn't just GameStop; it was a *rallying cry*.

As the ob-gyn swept back into the examining room, Sara quickly covered her phone with her palm, obscuring the screen.

She hadn't yet joined the GameStop battle; she was still just a lurker, an observer. But she was gathering up the nerve, day by day. Her Robinhood account hadn't thrown any confetti at her yet, but she knew that, sooner or later, she'd be ready.

The doctor reached the side of the table where Sara was lying and held up the picture he'd printed from the ultrasound, so she could see. The photo was dark, mostly blues and greens, but she could clearly make out the shape of her baby, tiny, growing inside her.

Sara felt herself starting to cry; she didn't know if she was happy, or sad, but for the first time in a long while, she felt—strong. The world was unfair, and the past year had been so hard. But now it felt like she was on the verge of writing her own way forward, and maybe, for once, she'd get to know what it felt like to be on the winning side.

Maybe, finally, it would be her turn.

CHAPTER ELEVEN

inning is not a sometime thing, it's an all-time thing.
Though Gabe Plotkin was firmly lodged in his rental home in Florida, having closed down the Madison Avenue offices of Melvin Capital as far back as March 13, as Covid had just begun its deadly march around the globe— whenever he closed his eyes, he was right back in Manhattan, moving through the empty corridors of his firm, passing the glass-walled, high-tech conference rooms and starkly appointed offices, the vacant trading desks and filing centers; and even in his mind's eye, none of it felt right.

You don't win once in a while; you don't do things right once in a while. You do them all the time.

He knew what was off because it was impossible to ignore: the silence. To him, that was one of the worst things about this pandemic year. Even before he'd left New York for Florida, it had bothered him to his core: how damn quiet everything was. The streets of the city twenty-two floors below his offices, which should have been packed with cars and taxis and buses jockeying for position, horns honking and curses flying, in the crowded traffic of a sunny, if frigid,

Tuesday afternoon. The sidewalks, which should have been packed with wave after wave of people; tourists loaded with shopping bags from the high-end stores lining Madison Avenue, businessmen and -women in suits with laptop bags, backpacks, and even the odd briefcase, all talking on their phones or shouting at the taxis while dodging hot dog vendors and halal carts. Even the plaza right outside his building's revolving glass front doors, which should have been crowded with congregants brandishing coffees and high-priced, skillfully constructed salads around Christie's Sculpture Garden, lit up and glowing as the hours shifted toward evening.

Winning is habit.

Instead, silence. The streets, sidewalks, and plaza were pretty much empty, like the Melvin offices. Although the traumatic early days of the pandemic, which had hit New York like a Category 5 hurricane—and who would ever forget the nights filled with ambulance sirens or the terrible pictures of hospitals overwhelmed by sick patients— had receded into a dull, exhaustingly numb drizzle of anxiety-laden moments of both optimism and never-ending dread, the bustle that made New York special still hadn't returned.

Like with most firms in the city, most of Melvin's employees were still working virtually, though some did scurry in and out of the offices from time to time, when the business of finance made it absolutely necessary. But apart from the odd, infrequent visitor, the offices remained a vacant shell; all the offices in all the skyscrapers remained vacant shells, like so many ghost ships floating by each other in a vast, windless sea.

To Gabe, such silence, and the distance that now existed between himself and his traders, was utterly unnatural. Melvin wasn't just a hedge fund, with its billions under management, populated by thirty-odd traders and their support staff. It was a family, made up of the very smartest, hardworking, most accomplished minds in the business, carefully curated by Gabe and his partners, sharing a single, noble purpose.

Winning is habit.

Gabe set his jaw, still imagining he was moving through his offices, the powerful words floating behind his eyes. When you walked into most Wall Street firms with billions of dollars on their books, you were greeted by millions of dollars of artwork hanging from their walls. Basquiats, Picassos, Warhols, Koons; sometimes you'd be chatting with a portfolio manager, and there would be a $30 million splash of color right behind his desk, hovering above his Bloomberg terminal.

But from the start, Gabe had built Melvin Capital to be different. When you walked into Melvin, you didn't see paintings; you saw inspirational quotes. When he'd first launched the company, there had been a single quote wall; now there were quotes everywhere. They'd cost Gabe nothing, but to Gabe, they meant more than any Picasso ever could.

Especially in times like this—when it wasn't just the pandemic that had his world turning strange and unnatural, the carpeted floor of his office seeming to rock beneath his feet—he could turn to the brilliant words of people like Vince Lombardi, the famed late coach of the Packers, one of the winningest figures in all of sports history—to keep him focused on the bottom line. From the beginning, Lombardi's words had captured the philosophy behind the fund Gabe had hoped to build: To be truly successful, a trader needed to understand that you had to work hard every day, and always do things the right way. Consistency trumped quick profits, and there were no shortcuts.

Growing up, Gabe had been obsessed not just with Lombardi, but with all of sports—football, basketball, but particularly baseball. So it was no surprise that he often likened what went on in the trading world to what happened on the playing fields. Some of his earliest memories were of reading the sports section of the Sunday newspaper and memorizing every statistic of every player; once, on a road trip to a Red Sox game with his father and his friends, Gabe had spent the ride correcting them as they got the stats wrong. To other kids, even the ones who loved baseball and basketball as much as Gabe did, those stats were just numbers. But Gabe had always known there was power in them. Current numbers and past numbers put together in just the right way predicted future numbers. And predicting future numbers was the main—and perhaps only—true business of a fund like Melvin.

In general, hedge funds were more backroom than boardroom. Despite the fact that they could be immensely large, they operated in secret, and they were reluctant to ever show their hand unless they were legally bound to do so. One of the few times a fund like Melvin let people in on their strategies was when they were first incorporated. Melvin had hit the Street as a long-short equity fund—a prominent investment approach that went back many years—built around intense research, modeling that could include hundreds of companies, followed literally for years, drilled down to the cornerstones of their headquarters, and a stable of trading professionals that would include the brightest and best of Wall Street.

And right out of the gate, Melvin had been a success. In 2015, they had run a 47 percent profit, placing them as the second most successful fund in the industry. By 2017, they had still been hitting 40 percent in profits. A bad 2018 had been followed by a huge 2019, and they had cemented themselves as one of the top performers in town. They'd grown a $1 billion bankroll—$200 million of which had been invested by Steve Cohen, Gabe's previous boss—to a fund now worth over $12.5 billion, combining long and short positions on a wide variety of stocks. Melvin's first year out, Gabe had focused on consumer companies, on which he'd been an expert at S.A.C. His positions had included Amazon, Foot Locker, Del Frisco's, Dick's Sporting Goods; and right out of the gate, he'd gone large, investing $900 million of his $1 billion under management.

And as a long-short fund, he'd also been obligated to take short positions—betting against companies—which was a tactic that, to most experts in finance, was uncontroversial. The thinking went, when companies were performing poorly, or were mismanaged, or were in an industry that was being overrun, or were simply likely to fail, taking a short position wasn't just logical—it protected the marketplace by pointing out overpriced stocks, prevented fraud by acting as a check against dubious management, and poked holes in potential bubbles. Short sellers also added liquidity and volume to a stock—because they were obligated to buy the stock back at some point in the future. Yes, short sellers profited when companies failed, but usually a short seller wasn't banking on a company failing—just that the stock's price would eventually correct toward its true valuation.

Sometimes, though, a trader picked up a short position because the company in question really *was* going to fail. Because, perhaps, it was in an industry that was dying; had management that seemed completely unable or unwilling to pivot; and had deep fundamental issues in its financing that seemed impossible to overcome.

Melvin Capital had become extremely adept at identifying just such companies. Although overall, most of Melvin's investments were long, many of its short positions had paid off handsomely. In its first year out of the gate, it had been reported that Melvin had made 70 percent of its profits from its short positions. And it was during this time period, at the very inception of his fund, that Gabe Plotkin had taken his first deep look into GameStop—and decided to go short.

At the time, it had been an uncomplicated and easy decision. In 2014, the stock had been trading at $40 a share. Gabe hadn't been alone in his position—many Wall Street firms had read the writing on the wall and seen what was happening to mall-based retail and overextended consumer franchises. GameStop had an archaic business model— selling new and used video games in physical stores, while the market was being overtaken by digital downloads via the Internet—and seemingly no forward strategy. Sure, they had some cash and inventory, and an interesting reach. But to survive, they'd need to reinvent themselves for the digital world. Gaming consoles of the future, most believed, were not going to use physical cartridges or CDs to go online.

They were a business in demise, and it looked as if they were going to burn all the way to the ground.

And burn they had—from $40 a share all the way to around $4, exactly as Gabe and much of Wall Street had predicted. And yet, the short interest hadn't fallen—in fact, it had increased. GameStop had proven that, at least as far as the market was concerned, the thing they were good at was failure. Even as the gaming industry ballooned, GameStop's profits decreased.

And then, the pandemic. Mall retail, already on shaky footing, cratered. Although one might argue that betting against a beloved mall franchise during a worldwide pandemic was ethically dubious, Melvin's mathematical-based reading of the situation had only gotten stronger. In 2020—even as the gaming industry had its best year ever, due to homebound customers playing video games round the clock, GameStop continued to lose money: they reported losses of $215.3 million, or $3.31 per share, on top of their 2019 loss of $470.9 million, or $5.38 per share.

The odds of GameStop recovering had only gotten worse. Likewise, the stock had continued to fall, all the way to $2.57 a share—then hovered back at around $5, and even so, shorts continued piling on.

Just as short selling GameStop had seemed the most obvious, ordinary, run-of-the-mill trade in 2014, Gabe might have assumed that adding more put options to his position in 2020, to leverage toward even bigger profits if the company finally collapsed, would be equally uncontroversial. The fact that option positions had to be reported on a Form 13F filing with the SEC, meaning they would be made public, wasn't particularly concerning either; even though hedge funds liked to keep their strategies secret, why would a 13F filing indicating positions that included as many as ninety-one different companies—standard practice in the industry—make any waves?

Certainly, he couldn't have predicted that a bunch of anonymous people congregating on a subreddit board called WallStreetBets would suddenly single Melvin out, to represent all of the short sellers taking aim at GameStop. Nor could he have imagined that he himself would suddenly end up being commented on, made fun of, even threatened on WSB, on Discord—another social network frequented by the Reddit crowd—and even in messages sent directly to his company.

At first, the social media chatter around GameStop had been largely innocuous. The posts on social media had been infrequent, mostly isolated, and largely about how much individual retail investors liked the stock and were making money investing in it. But as the fall progressed toward winter, the tenor of the posts began to change.

The posts became more and more personal and targeted—such as the infamous Chernobyl video, predicting the explosion of Gabe's firm. Although Gabe understood that the WSB board trafficked in dark humor and dramatic license, it was hard to see the humor in a lot of what was suddenly going on surrounding GameStop and Melvin's short position, and specifically, Gabe himself. Some of the comments he'd seen had been steeped in anti-Semitism and hate—It's very clear we need a second holocaust, the Jews can't keep getting away with this—and he himself had begun to receive similarly racist and derogatory texts. Where before, the comments on social media had been largely about buying GameStop because the commenters liked the stock, the narrative had shifted, to buying GameStop as a way to attack Melvin Capital's short position. And throughout, there was an easily seen subtext in many of these posts that pitted Gabe himself as some sort of evil figure to be destroyed.

Gabe wasn't thin-skinned. He'd made his bones on Wall Street, a place notorious for profanity, off-color personalities, and fight-or-die philosophies. Though he kept a low profile in public, he was known by many in the industry for being extremely likable, a good guy, who could also be aggressive and intense. And it would be a lie for him to describe himself as unemotional; he had the competitive spirit of an athlete, and as the quote went, for him, *winning was an all-time thing*.

But the hateful, racist comments, and the vicious memes predicting his company's fall, were hard to ignore. Quite the opposite—they were the kind of thing that could light the competitive spirit in someone who played the game at the level he did.

He wasn't thrilled that the Reddit mob knew about his short position—but that didn't change the fact that it was the *correct* play. The stock had gone up since its $5 plateau. But that didn't change the company's fundamentals. It was still a flailing business in a dying industry. The math was in Gabe's favor, and if there was one thing he'd learned to trust, it was math.

Not only did he continue to believe in the short play— but in the initial days, he added to it: an additional 600,000 shares via put options for the ending quarter of 2020— around $130 million in value. This was on top of the shares he had shorted; and the 13F and any public documents only revealed the tip of the iceberg. Nobody could really know how big a short position Gabe had taken—only that he was now risking a significant portion of his fund on this single bet.

Other firms might have considered such a move risky; shorting meant the potential losses were endless. And the short volume on GameStop was immense—well beyond Melvin's gamble—and was now being reported as nearing *140* percent of the float. That such a thing was even possible—that 40 percent more shares of a stock could be short than actually *existed*—seemed contradictory. But Gabe could take it as more evidence that his view was sound. So many people on Wall Street knew this company was going down that they were willing to borrow and borrow and borrow shares to sell short—so many shares that almost half were being borrowed more than once.

No number of angry posts on Reddit could change the fact that the smart money was on the short side. And it was unlikely—if not impossible—that a stock could get disconnected from its fundamentals simply by being pushed by retail day traders.

WallStreetBets wasn't populated by professionals—it was mostly amateurs, gamblers, hell, they called *themselves* "retards," "apes," and "degenerates," terms that disturbed Gabe, and that he would never use. Some of them appeared to be doing real due diligence—but did they really believe they could dislodge a ticker from a company, somehow turn a stock into some sort of token, like bitcoin or doge?

In the deeper corners of Gabe's mind, maybe he knew that what was spurring him on wasn't entirely math, but also his competitive nature. He'd never put it like this himself, but plenty of others in the industry would: Gabe was a winner—and these little shits on their couches tossing off angry memes onto Reddit were losers. And they were going to learn a very painful lesson.

Wherever the stock was, it was going to go down. GameStop was a melting ice cube. The WSB board could post all they wanted; shit-talking, after all, was a part of every sport. But Gabe Plotkin knew that time was on his side.

A melting ice cube always ended up the same—a nice big puddle of water.

PART TWO

"We like the stock! We like the stock!"
—Jim Cramer

"Gamestonk!!"
—Elon Musk

CHAPTER TWELVE

January 11, 2021

Keith Gill's left boot touched the black ice first, the sole slipping against the frictionless surface, sending his entire left leg out in front of him in a bizarre angle that would have brought him right down to the sidewalk if he hadn't been holding his daughter's gloved hand in his own. She was laughing as he used her weight to anchor himself, and he was laughing, too, but not only because their morning walk around the block had just turned into a circus show; he was still looking at the screen on the phone in his other hand, even though the balancing act of checking the stock news report while guiding his daughter along the poorly shoveled sidewalks of Wilmington was as treacherous as any race he'd ever run.

Even more difficult than keeping his poise on that special brand of New England ice was reading a financial news report, complete with SEC filings, on three inches of screen. He supposed he could have updated the phone during his Christmas trip home to his family; but having surplus money in his bank account was such a weird and new experience. The thought that he could afford something as benign as a new phone was both thrilling and frightening; even though he felt certain it was the result of deep research and due diligence, it still seemed like such an unlikely turn of events.

It had been a month now since Keith Gill had officially become a millionaire. He was the first in his family to be able to say that, and it had happened because of one wild YOLO trade. Most of it was still on paper—although the phrase needed to be updated, because who the hell used paper anymore—but the $53,000 he'd put into GameStop had ballooned into a figure seven digits long.

As he steadied himself while using his thumb to scroll deeper into the news report, his smile widened. A million dollars was a life-changing number—but Keith hadn't changed his life much, yet. Still, he had finally told his entire family what he'd been up to, during his Christmas visit home. Everyone had been supportive, although they might have still thought him crazy. His mother had only asked if what he was doing was illegal in any way. He'd patiently explained to her that making money on a stock, no matter how unlikely, was one of the most legal, and to be frank, patriotic things one could do. The fact that he had been talking about his trade—ad nauseum—online, to anyone who would listen, didn't make it any less kosher.

And it was true, his Roaring Kitty livestreams had morphed well beyond the few-minute segments he had planned, to marathon sessions lasting late into the night. His longest had tapped out at over seven hours, though anyone who had stuck through the entire thing had to have been crazier than Keith. And his audience had grown; he was now one of the more popular posters on the WSB board, and whenever he put up one of his YOLO updates, he was certain to get a storm of comments. He didn't just have fans, he had disciples, and a fair number of them were obviously buying GameStop themselves. But he believed—or at least wanted to believe—that they were all buying with their eyes wide open. He had made it clear, often and always, that the stock market was risky, and his YOLO style, even riskier. The enormous short float on GameStop was evidence that most of the experts still believed the stock was a dog.

From Keith's point of view, it was a dog with a lot of bark. When he'd opened the news app on his phone, halfway into his walk with his daughter, it was that bark that had almost sent him to the sidewalk. His current thesis about the stock had been pretty simple; there was more opportunity for good news than bad, since all the bad was already baked in. And with such immense short pressure, from Melvin and others, every bit of good news would push the price upward. A hundred and forty percent short shares meant that if the stock started to run, the short sellers would be on the hook for 80 million shares, and there were more like 60 million in existence. From the Reddit board, it appeared that a not insignificant portion of those shares were in the "diamond" hands of people like Keith, who would rather sell their grandparents than their GameStop.

Keith's grin multiplied. *Fall in love with a stock?* He'd already married it, had kids, and was planning his grandchildren's weddings. Which was why the news that had just broken across his phone was so monumental.

The announcement had come from GameStop and been parroted across financial media: Ryan Cohen and a couple members of his Chewy crew were joining the GameStop board. Already, Cohen owned a significant stake in the company—on top of the 5 percent of the float first revealed in his filing back in August, he'd added his way to 10 percent in November, a position valued at over $79 million at the time. That addition of shares had been followed by an aggressive letter to the company's management, pointing out everything they'd been doing wrong, and demanding that they pivot toward online gaming, build up their e-presence, and try some innovative strategies, such as getting into eSports, streaming, and mobile apps. At the time, GameStop hadn't seemed overly receptive to an agitating outsider. But today's news was a complete one-eighty; Ryan Cohen was riding in like a white knight to save the company, and now Keith would be eating tendies and drinking beer on his livestream that evening, because Cohen on the board meant there was a real chance he could help reinvent the company, the same way he'd reinvented the pet food business.

Keith was walking faster now, and his daughter was skipping over the ice to keep up. He could see from his phone that the stock was already coasting toward $20 a share on the news. He wasn't sure it could hit a new twelve-month high—it had danced around $21 a share in late December— but still, there was plenty of potential upside.

In the back of Keith's mind, visions of the beginnings of the fabled "short squeeze" the WSB board continuously crowed about sparked to life—but he didn't want to get ahead of himself. He'd tried to stay above the more aggressive story lines on the site, the ones that pitted the GameStop believers against the hedge funds, particularly the ones that made it personal between him and Melvin Capital. He didn't know anything about Melvin Capital, he certainly didn't know Gabe Plotkin, and he was pretty sure they traveled in very different circles. If Plotkin had ever driven through Brockton, he'd likely have kept the windows closed and the doors locked.

But short squeeze or not, Keith believed that GameStop, the company that had already made him a millionaire, was about to have another moment.

He looked down at his daughter and saw that she was still laughing because he'd almost fallen. One day, when she was old enough to understand, he would explain. Momentum was a wave that could sweep the stablest racer right off his feet.

CHAPTER THIRTEEN

January 13, 2021

This is gonna hurt me more than it's gonna hurt you, Kim thought to herself as the female tech—all smiles beneath her mask—came at her with the needle. The sleeve of Kim's scrubs were up around her shoulder, and she was in one of the little curtained booths at the back of the nurses' area, which they sometimes used to dispense medicine—but today, the place was about as private as a train station. The curtain was pulled back and the entire nursing staff, along with the orderlies, was gathered to watch. Chinwe had his phone out and two of the girls were using an iPad to get their own image, which they'd eventually print out and put on the board—right next to the shot they'd taken of the walker imbedded in the partition from weeks ago, which was now displayed under the comical title: "PT Eval Passed."

"If I turn into an alligator, I'm coming for all of you."

The needle went in, and thankfully, Kim didn't feel a thing. She waved her other arm, taking in a smattering of applause. The moment was surprisingly emotional; Kim had never been overly panicked about Covid—she dealt with it every day and had even done shifts in the Covid ward upstairs—but this was still a significant moment.

There had never been any question: she was going to be the first on the staff to get the vaccine. There was a surprising amount of hesitancy among her colleagues, even though they were medical professionals and had seen the misery caused by the virus firsthand. But Kim felt it her responsibility to influence the others with her behavior. If watching her made even one of them more comfortable with taking that first step toward everything getting back to normal, she was happy to be the hospital's guinea pig.

She thanked the tech, who was busy pressing a Band-Aid over the injection site. Then she was up and smiling.

Chinwe and Kamal continued their applause as she passed them on her way toward the break room. She knew she had to stick close for fifteen minutes, but she figured the break room was good enough. If she started to grow a tail or claws, she'd still be within shouting distance. As she went, she fought the urge to give Chinwe a hug; too soon, she figured, though if the shot was as good as they said it was, maybe soon the term "social distancing" would recede from everyone's vocabulary. Kim couldn't wait until it was just another shared linguistic memory. Along with "flattening the curve" and "contact tracing" and "herd immunity."

And maybe even "GameStop," Kim added to herself as she pushed through the double doors, already reaching toward her phone, which was tucked in the pockets of her scrubs. The twenty minutes she'd spent waiting for the shot had already been the longest she'd gone that day without checking her Robinhood account or WallStreetBets; but now that she had fifteen minutes to kill before she could head home to her kids, she was ready to dive back into the madness.

She was completely lost in her phone's screen by the time she reached the quiet of the break room, dropping into her usual seat at the round table by the door. Someone had brought donuts in honor of the vaccine—a mixed, colorful selection that rose like a sprinkled metropolis above a pair of plastic cafeteria trays. But the pastries, no matter how tempting, couldn't compete with what Kim was seeing on her phone.

Her investment in GameStop had doubled in a single day: the price had shot up past $31 a share. Kim had already read through many of the comments on WallStreetBets, and had even watched some of Roaring Kitty's latest livestream; she knew all about the addition of the Chewy guys to the GameStop board. But she didn't think a change in leadership alone could account for what was happening to the stock. She'd had a million bosses in her life, and no matter how brilliant or innovative they thought themselves, they'd never made much of a difference to her day-to-day.

A trio of new board members, no matter how many bags of dog food they'd sold, weren't going to make a stock double. But there it was, in glowing numbers and rapidly rising graphs. Kim had made over $1600 in the past twenty-four hours.

Her cheeks felt hot as she went from WallStreetBets back to her account; she was so swept up in the moment, she didn't notice that Chinwe was suddenly hovering over her shoulder.

"They find another batch of ballots under a bridge?"

He took the seat next to her, rubbing the Band-Aid on

his own shoulder with one hand, while reaching for a donut from the tower with the other. Jelly, powdered, and he took such a delicate bite that normally Kim would have fired some snarky comment back at him, but she was in too good a mood.

"Better than a box of ballots."

She showed him the phone, and his eyes widened.

"Thirty-one forty? That's impossible."

"I think it's happening."

"The Melvin Capital thing."

Chinwe gave her the same look he'd given her the last time they'd had this conversation, just a day earlier. She'd been trying to find different ways to explain what the posters on WallStreetBets believed was about to happen, mainly because she'd been trying to understand it herself. She figured she'd give it one more go—after all, she still had plenty of time to kill. The key was to find a way to make it simple.

She thought for a moment, watching Chinwe gingerly attacking his donut, then smiled.

"Let's say that donut is GameStop stock," she started.

"Does it have to be *this* donut?"

"Yes, it does. And let's say the current market price for that donut is five dollars. And I'm Melvin Capital. I think that donut is garbage. So I borrow it from you."

She took the donut out of his hand. He looked at her, but she just kept smiling.

"We make an agreement that I have to give the donut back to you in a couple of days—"

"Kim."

"So I sell the donut into the market, for five dollars, the current price."

She returned the donut to the tray.

"I took a bite out of that."

"And I wait," she continued. "Planning to buy it back and return it to you when the price goes down, pocketing the difference. But let's say the price doesn't go down. Because other people love these donuts, and they've started buying them like crazy."

She starts to take donuts off the tray, putting them to the side.

"And buying them and buying them. Maybe a piece of news comes out, something about how donuts cure Covid. The price spikes a little higher. And people just keep buying them."

The tray was now half empty, the donuts piled up on either side.

"And these buyers, maybe they're not just your average donut lovers. Maybe they hang out on some wild Reddit board talking about how rich people, who get to the donut store early, have been screwing them out of the good flavors forever. About how this time, they aren't going to let these rich people push them around."

She grabs more donuts from the tray.

"Now I still owe you that donut I borrowed. But it's not just me—it's all of my friends on Wall Street, too. They've all borrowed donuts. Some of them, reading the writing on the wall, start to buy them back to make good on their debt."

She takes a couple more donuts, puts them to the side.

"Which makes the price go up even faster. But my friends have no choice now. Like me, they still need to return those donuts."

She keeps taking donuts until there is only one left, the jelly donut that she'd first borrowed from Chinwe.

"The price of donuts has gone through the roof, but a whole bunch of us still haven't covered. What do you think happens when we all try to get that last donut at the same time?"

"Don't," Chinwe warned.

"You know I have to."

Kim gave the donut a good squeeze. Jelly oozed out from every side. Chinwe sighed.

"But it's worse than that," Kim said. "Because not only did my friends and I borrow every donut in the box, we borrowed more donuts than were ever in the box. If this continues, pretty soon the short sellers will be trying to grab for donuts that don't even exist."

Chinwe reached past her, finding a new, unsqueezed donut, moving it far out of her reach.

"Now what happens?" he asked. "The price keeps going up forever?"

She shrugged. Chinwe shook his head.

"You doubled your money. That's good. You should sell."

"Aren't you listening? The donuts—"

"We're not talking about donuts."

They'd had many conversations about their finances over the years they'd worked together, about how hard their jobs could be, about how difficult planning a future could seem on an RN's salary. And she knew, on the face of it, he was right: she was up $1600, not yet enough to pay for Brian's braces, but that kind of money would cover a lot of bills.

Still, watching the price continue to rise, reading all the comments on WSB—it really did feel like the squeeze was either happening, or about to happen. If the diamond hands stood firm . . .

"You can't beat these guys," Chinwe said, as if reading her thoughts. "This is a casino, and they're the house. They'll find a way to win. They always do."

Chinwe was usually the one telling *her* to have faith.

"David beat Goliath," she finally responded.

"This isn't David versus Goliath. It's David versus Goliath, and Goliath's cousin, and Goliath's best friend."

Kim shook her head.

"There are a lot of us, too."

Chinwe sighed again, then went back to his donut. Kim watched him take another little bite. She knew he was just trying to help, but he wasn't seeing what she was seeing. Battle lines had been drawn.

It was easy to think of WallStreetBets as a disjointed, chaotic gathering place for fools and gamblers, because that's how they often portrayed themselves. But Chinwe didn't understand: the fools and gamblers had come together in a common cause, and there was great power in that sort of unity. Anger was a powerful motivator, far stronger than greed. Kim had seen it in the election of 2016, and Chinwe's blindness to it had cost him $100. Melvin Capital and their colleagues on Wall Street were proving to be just as blind, grievously underestimating the army they were up against.

Kim had no intention of selling. If anything, she was thinking of buying *more*.

"Goliath thinks that he's the hero of the story," she said as she watched Chinwe eat his donut. "Right until the rock hits him in the face."

CHAPTER FOURTEEN

January 19, 2021

There once was a stock that put to sea,
The name of the stock was GME,
The price blew up and the shorts dipped down,
Hold my bully boys hold.

Soon may the Tendieman come,
To send our rocket into the sun,
One day when the trading is done,
We'll take our gains and go...

Jeremy's eyes were closed, his bare feet tapping against the carpet beneath his desk, as the image of a three-masted sailing vessel set against a black background undulated in perfect rhythm to the sea shanty that he'd already set to memory, even though he'd only stumbled upon the post—dropped onto WallStreetBets by a user calling himself or herself quigonshin—that very morning. It was no wonder that *The Tendieman* was fast going viral among the growing Reddit army; Jeremy himself was fighting the urge to click over to the meme and listen to it for the hundredth time, and if he hadn't been on a date that very moment, he would have given in to the urge.

To be fair, describing Jeremy's latest attempt to make a connection with a human of the opposite sex as a "date" would be an extreme act of creative license. Even if the engagement hadn't involved Zoom, and a crappy wireless connection on her side running headlong into his obvious preoccupation with the other windows still open on his laptop—particularly, WallStreetBets and his trading account—it still would have been going poorly.

Jeremy had also been fairly competent at dating; especially, in the physical world, he'd become a master at decrypting the signs that a date wasn't going well. He was able to read the cues like he was cracking his own personal Da Vinci Code. Little things, like the way his date's phone would somehow end up on the table next to her dinner, so she could see the texts popping up from her friends. Or the way she'd search the restaurant for the waiter almost the moment their desserts had arrived. More often than not, he could be charming enough to land a second outing, but sometimes he had to be prepared for that speech he'd get, between the check and the Uber home: *about how great it was to find someone you could just talk to, someone you knew was going to end up such a great friend...*

But in this year of Zoom, it was agonizingly difficult to know what anyone was really thinking. Sure, Jeremy had counted a dozen awkward silences before he'd started replaying GameStop sea shanties in his head; but awkward silences were common during virtual chats, and it was hard to distinguish true discomfort from wireless glitches and

inadvertent mutes. It wasn't really until he'd started noticing his date's eyes shifting to whatever else was open on
her own computer that he knew for sure, the main thing
they had in common was their disinterest in continuing the
conversation, even if both of them were too polite to fumble
toward a good reason to sign off.

Jeremy supposed he was mostly to blame. He'd met
Teresa—the pretty sable-haired classmate filling up a square
on his laptop screen, which he'd moved all the way to the
bottom left corner, as close to the Esc key that his computer's design would allow—at the tail end of his freshman
year. She'd been dating a mutual acquaintance from one of
Jeremy's statistics classes, who'd ended up transferring to a
college in the Northeast. After Teresa's boyfriend had left,
she and Jeremy had struck up a deeper friendship, which
had led to a few late nights at a local diner, sharing exciting conversations about *probability biases*, *analytics*, and
reversion to the mean. Not exactly *Casablanca*, but when
they'd lost touch over the summer between freshman and
sophomore years, Jeremy had always wondered if there had
been some spark he'd just been missing.

Now he had his answer. It was Teresa who had first
reached out to him just a week earlier, inviting him for a
drink to reconnect. As intrigued as Jeremy had been, he'd
recoiled at the idea of meeting in person and had offered up
the Zoom call instead. From the start, it had pretty much
been a disaster. Without freshman statistics to fall back on,
they'd had very little to anchor a conversation around. And
for Jeremy, the timing couldn't have been worse. To say he
was preoccupied by what was going on with GameStop, and
his trading account, would have been a vast understatement.

Even before the Zoom call, he'd been staring at his laptop screen since he'd awoken from a fitful sleep at five in the morning, and he planned to stay rooted there, behind his desk, until hunger or some other equally important bodily function dragged him away.

She had not been two weeks from shore,
When Ryan Cohen joined the board,
The captain called all hands and swore,
He'll take his shares and hold.

Soon may the Tendieman come,
To send our rocket into the sun,
One day when the trading is done
We'll take our gains and go...

He really did feel like the song and its lyrics captured the feeling of hope that was sweeping through the Reddit board. And now that Jeremy was part of that mob, fully invested in GameStop, he felt like he was on the front lines, aligned with the rest of the degenerates in the battle that had obviously just begun.

He'd made his first purchase of the stock shortly after that day on the golf course with his father. Two hundred shares at an average price of $15.44, for $3,088—zero commission, of course. On January fourth, he'd added another 150 shares for $19.20, for another $2,880. A total investment of almost $6,000. From what he'd read on WallStreetBets, that put him near the middle of the pack, nowhere near legends like DFV but a loyal warrior in the fight.

And that's exactly how Jeremy had begun to see his trade:

not an investment, not even a YOLO swing for the moon, as he'd described it to his father. Once he'd actually taken the leap and bought shares, he'd become emotionally aligned with the WSB community in their quest to take on Wall Street.

Opening his eyes, doing his best to focus on the Zoom chat that was taking up as little of his laptop's real estate as he could respectfully justify, Jeremy wondered what Teresa would have thought if he'd told her about WallStreetBets, and the fact that he was now part of this movement revolving around a video game store and a guy in a bandanna on YouTube. Maybe she'd have heard about GameStop already—stories were already making their way into the business press, and it was only a matter of time before they'd reach the more mainstream news outlets. Though it was still a matter of debate whether a true short squeeze was beginning, the stock motion had been insane—just a few hours ago, Jeremy had watched the price reach $43. That meant his shares were now worth upwards of $15,000. He'd more than doubled his stake.

As good as Jeremy was doing in GameStop, his father was doing even better. After their conversation on the golf course, his dad had decided to follow him into the trade, and had bought 1000 shares at an average price of around $17. Compared to what Jeremy had risked, that was real money: a $17,000 investment that was now worth $43,000. Jeremy knew he was going to have to work hard to get his dad to continue to hold on to those shares. His dad only laughed whenever Jeremy brought up the term "diamond hands," and it was clear his dad was not approaching this with the same emotional fervor as Jeremy himself. Which, his dad had argued, was a good thing.

Jeremy would be the first to admit he had to be careful not to let himself get carried away. Already he was having trouble concentrating on his schoolwork, and he'd missed two study sessions with his "bubble" in the past few days. He'd started and stopped his latest problem set more than once, but linear algebra just didn't hold the same appeal as the war he was helping wage against Wall Street.

Maybe the girl on his Zoom had already heard a little about the war; if she'd turned on CNBC or read any business threads on Twitter that morning, for instance, she'd have already gotten a full serving of how the other side saw what was happening. Even though the price was still relatively earthbound, at $43, the suits and ties had already begun firing back. Maybe the most angering of the conservative voices striking out at the Reddit crew so far had to be the short-selling aficionado and activist Andrew Left, who ran a company called Citron Research. That very morning, right after the market had opened and GameStop had started to rise, Left's firm had put up a tweet advertising that tomorrow they were going to do a livestream: *The 5 reasons GameStop $GME buyers at these levels are the suckers at this poker game. Stock back to $20 fast. We understand short interest better than you and will explain.*

As one would expect, the tweet had hit WallStreetBets like a stick of dynamite. The community had immediately rallied together, going after Citron and Left in the manner of their medium. Vicious memes, personal attacks, ridicule—*squeeze the lemon*—nothing had been off-limits. Although Jeremy didn't condone some of the darker tactics employed by those who saw Citron on par with Melvin, an enemy to be destroyed, it was clear that Citron had little respect for the retail traders on WSB. To Jeremy, he was just some guy spewing his opinion, which was no more valid than DFV's. CNBC gave him a megaphone, but all he was really doing was galvanizing the opposition. By the end of the day, the online uproar would grow so intense, Citron would cancel its livestream—later claiming that its Twitter feed had been hacked.

Jeremy didn't agree with the vicious, personal attacks hurled at Left, but he did understand the WSB community's natural response to being called "suckers"—especially while the stock soared to new heights. And why should any of them listen to Left over DFV? Because he'd gone to a better college? Because he worked at a desk in Manhattan instead of out of a basement somewhere in Massachusetts?

Still, even if Teresa had been following GameStop, Jeremy would never have a chance to dazzle her with his trading account—because she was already halfway into an excuse about her laptop's battery running low. Jeremy wasn't sure which of them won the race to the Leave Meeting button, but in the frozen image of her face that remained on his screen just a moment too long, he could see that she shared his sense of relief.

Before the news had hit the market,
WallStreetBets came up and bought it,
With diamond hands they knew they'd profit,
If they could only hold.

Soon may the Tendieman come,
To send our rocket into the sun,
One day when the trading is done,
We'll take our gains and go…

He was already banishing Zoom back to his app folder when a new chime told him that he wasn't yet going to be allowed back to WallStreetBets, to the sea shanties and anti-Citron rants. A quick glance at his phone told him that his brother was FaceTiming—an accurate bit of timing that only a younger brother could pull off. Of course, Casper had known the date would end early and in failure. They had, after all, grown up sharing forty-four feet of canvas on a catamaran for much of their formative years.

Jeremy grudgingly accepted the call, to see Casper grinning widely at him from beneath his own mop of reddish-blond hair.

"You blew it again, right?"

"Shut up, dumbass."

"It's that sort of attitude that chases them away. Have you tried being nice?"

Jeremy reached for the screen to disconnect, and Casper waved his hands in front of his camera.

"Hold on man, just kidding. I didn't really call to talk about your ineptitude with the ladies. Dad texted me. About GameStop."

Jeremy's stomach dropped.

"He didn't sell, did he?"

There was a brief pause, which Casper milked for all it was worth.

"No. But I told him he should. And you should, too. Forty-three dollars a share! You're fucking rich!"

Jeremy exhaled.

"You don't know what you're talking about. This is just getting started."

Jeremy had already gone back and forth with Casper

about GameStop a handful of times, beginning during the long drive back from Christmas break. Casper had thought Jeremy was crazy and had given him a hard time about getting their dad to throw money in, as well.

"You're an expert now?"

"No," Jeremy said. "I'm an ape. I'm king of the apes."

His brother was not impressed.

"You really think these Wall Street firms who are shorting the hell out of GME don't know what they're doing?"

Jeremy didn't think his brother really wanted an answer, but Jeremy had given the subject a lot of thought. He didn't know much about Melvin Capital, other than that it was one of the most respected firms on the Street. And Gabe Plotkin was supposed to be this rock star trader, groomed by Steve Cohen, one of the most feared men in finance. Plotkin was smart, probably smarter than everyone on the WallStreetBets board. But, Jeremy believed, Plotkin didn't understand what he was up against.

He decided to put it in terms his brother might understand. His brother didn't invest in stocks, but he'd played a lot of poker, with his friends at school and also online. He knew how to gamble, and he knew what it meant to get too cocky.

"Melvin is holding a pair of aces. And the flop has hit, and it's showing two sixes and another ace. Melvin is certain they've won with their full house, aces over sixes. What they don't see is us. We're holding a pair of sixes—we've got four of a kind. Melvin and the other Wall Street firms are making the right play, shorting a company they believe is a dog. But they're still going to lose. And they're so damn arrogant, so used to winning, they just can't let it go."

His brother paused, digesting it, then looked into his camera.

"I guess you're not going to sell."

"Maybe I'm never going to sell."

"That's stupid. It's GameStop. Its market value is already—"

"And that's what you, and Wall Street, don't understand. You still think the market value means something. You sound like Citron, going on CNBC telling me why I'm the sucker at the table. You don't get what's really happening here."

"Jeremy."

"The whole world is screwed up," Jeremy continued. He felt his face heating up, his emotions flowing. "We're all stuck at home on our couches and in our beds, and these Wall Street guys like Citron and Melvin are looking at us from their beach houses and their penthouse apartments. And they've got teams of analysts and complicated mathematical algorithms and huge bankrolls, and what have we got?"

Casper paused again.

"God, that date must have been bad—"

"We've got GME," Jeremy finished.

And then he did reach for the screen, and disconnected.

GME. Not GameStop—GME.

A once-in-a-lifetime shot at the moon.

CHAPTER FIFTEEN

January 22, 2021

Orlando, Florida.
A sunny, breezy, beautiful Friday afternoon.
Ten minutes before market close.

Jim Swartwout caught his breath for the first time since breakfast, as his gaze settled on the swaying fronds of a distant palm tree through the windows of his corner office in Robinhood's Lake Mary, Orlando, headquarters. He let the last few beats until the closing bell tick away in silence, just breathing, deeply in tune with those undulating, scythe-shaped leaves. Willing his way toward the end of one of the most unusual days—capping one of the most unusual weeks—of his year-and-a-half tenure at the Silicon Valley upstart brokerage.

To be fair, if you could say anything about the company's satellite offices in sunny, breezy, beautiful Lake Mary, it was that *unusual* things almost never happened there. The whole reason you opened headquarters in this sun-bleached splash of land twenty miles up I-4 from downtown Orlando was to avoid *action*. Lake Mary wasn't just sleepy; it was delightfully comatose, a wealthy latticework of beautiful homes set around natural reserves, lakes, biking trails, open-air restaurants, boutiques, good school systems, whose main selling point was its proximity to the airport and that it squatted in the shadow of the biggest tourist destination on earth. That shadow had mouse ears, but even so, Lake Mary was a wonderful place to raise a family, and a fairly *odd* place to put the beating heart of the hottest, most disruptive company in fintech.

Of course, the decision to open a satellite office among the palm trees and alligator-infested waterways of Northern Florida had much to do with the complex, cost-benefit calculations that went along with rapid, breakneck expansion; Robinhood was growing so fast, and hiring so many, it made sense that they would expand, geographically, well beyond Menlo Park. Plans would soon be announced for offices in New York and Seattle—but Lake Mary had come first, initially announced in 2017 with the heady goal of employing 200. Compared to the thousands who worked at your average investment bank in the bevy of skyscrapers sprouting from lower Manhattan, where Jim had previously been employed, or for that matter, the 77,000 who toiled in the glow of Cinderella's Castle at the Magic Kingdom just down the highway, it was a baby step. But for a Silicon Valley start-up aimed primarily at millennials with a few thousand bucks of barely disposable income to toss at the stock market on a random Friday afternoon, it was quite impressive.

No less impressive, the Lake Mary headquarters themselves; maybe not as magazine-worthy as the beachy sprawl in Menlo Park, but fresh and modern, with state-of-the-art conference rooms and offices, and of course, plenty of windows. There was also the mural, similar to Menlo, with its cats and nods to Sherwood, but in Lake Mary, the forest had been exchanged for a dock-filled coastal bay, complete with motorboats, lounge chairs, feline pirates, and alligators wearing sunglasses. Camera ready, for whenever Vlad and Baiju visited—though the two unicorns didn't come through Lake Mary very often.

Jim wasn't complaining—and who could complain, this close to Space Mountain—but as with most tech companies centered in the valley whose tentacles reached beyond the California state borders, Robinhood's satellite offices didn't often get front billing. It was easy to think of the Lake Mary operation as something hidden behind a geographic curtain, and Jim himself was usually a voice on the other end of a phone—or more recently, a face on the other side of a Zoom—someone you only heard, or saw, when things went wrong. But Jim knew better; Robinhood wasn't like other Silicon Valley tech companies, because it wasn't just a *tech* company. And Jim's team in Lake Mary—already seventy strong, growing day by day since he'd joined in June 2019—was at the core of the business Robinhood was building, and part of the reason that Robinhood would soon be worth many multiples of the $4 billion valuation that had recently been bandied about in the pages of numerous financial papers.

Still, being at the center of what Robinhood was striving to be—the "fin" in its fintech—didn't mean Jim's position at the company could be described as something particularly flashy, nor was he himself as sparkly and glittery as Vlad or Baiju, who seemed to have been artfully crafted for some future cover of *Forbes*. It didn't help that the role Jim had first been hired to fill—head of clearing—wasn't the sort of title you could easily explain at a dinner party. To be sure, there weren't many dinner parties in Lake Mary, but if Jim had showed up dressed as Goofy or wearing rodent ears, at least people would have had some idea what he did for a living. Now that he was president of the company and the chief operating officer, it was a little easier to describe himself over cocktails; but when he got into the nitty-gritty, it still often seemed like he'd willingly entered some sort of financial witness protection program.

Jim hadn't started out in clearing. He'd been a trader on Wall Street before shifting toward the entrepreneurial, tech side of the business. He'd run the trading desk at E-Trade, one of the earliest online brokerages, back in 1999, and after becoming COO of that company, he'd moved on to a similar position at Scottrade, then to president of trade-MONSTER. On top of that, over the years, he'd worked at numerous financial institutions, and had been in and out of many start-ups. But being part of Robinhood was a dream situation, for a couple of reasons.

Robinhood was unique among its peers, for having built out its own clearing platform using brand-new, cloud-based technology, planting itself squarely at the intersection of technology and finance. And on top of that, Robinhood's mission was unique and inspiring; the company wasn't just profit-oriented and profitable—but to Jim, it seemed *morally* good. Robinhood wanted to level the playing field by opening up trading to average people, many of whom had never had the opportunity to invest in stocks before. When Robinhood had opened its doors, 50 percent of stocks were owned by the top 1 percent; if simplifying a trading platform brought equity to the markets, it was an enormous net positive.

But as slick and shiny as that platform might be, Jim knew that the real magic was beneath the gloss—in the piping that made Robinhood work. And that piping was Jim's domain. Robinhood was reinventing the stock market for millennials and Gen Z, but the last thing young people wanted to see or think about was the piping that made it all work. And sometimes, to the outside observer, maybe it could appear that a similar attitude extended all the way to Menlo Park. You didn't get more "arm's length" from Silicon Valley than Orlando without hitting ocean. And the attitude made sense; you might carry on a pleasant conversation with the plumber while he was fixing your sink, but you didn't often invite him to dinner afterward.

But this past week—culminating in this crazy Friday afternoon—was one of those rare moments when the plumber hung around, at least until the main course. Jim had been on the phone with Menlo Park a number of times over the past few hours. What was going on in the market, and particularly on Robinhood, wasn't an emergency—but it was concerning, and more than that, it was strange. Because unlike other market issues that popped up from time to time, involving clearing and capital attention, this situation didn't concern a variety of unusual trading surrounding a large number of the 13,000 equities bought and sold by Robinhood customers. This situation mostly revolved around a single stock.

As the head of clearing and now the COO, Jim had faced his fair share of difficult circumstances having to do with customers and trading. There had been a couple of speed bumps, some before he'd joined the company—like the alleged confusion involving banking regulations surrounding Robinhood's saving accounts back in 2018—and more recent issues, like a $65 million SEC fine revolving around the company's alleged lack of communication about their payment for order flow practices. But the most difficult moment by far had taken place only seven months earlier when a twenty-year-old college kid named Alexander Kearns had committed suicide after seeing a temporary negative balance of over $730,000 in his Robinhood account. Although Kearns had not actually been on the hook for the immense loss, which was the result of some complicated put options—and he may not have realized that the negative balance would soon be erased by a credit to his account—it was clear the confusion of the moment had weighed heavily on the boy. Kearns's suicide note had read, in part, as reported by *Forbes* magazine after Kearns's death: "How was a 20 year old with no income able to get assigned almost a million dollars' worth of leverage?"

For everyone at Robinhood, this had been an immense, emotional, and tragic moment, which had also flashed all over the news and gained traction across many social networks. Robinhood had done what it could in the aftermath to make sure that such a misunderstanding couldn't occur again—improving the site's messaging involving options trading, making changes to its interface, and expanding their educational content, especially surrounding options and margin trading. Such a tragedy should never have happened, and Jim and the rest of the company's leadership would do everything they could to try and safeguard their customers going forward.

But Jim knew that powerful trading tools such as options —
which gave users the ability to leverage themselves — would
always carry some level of risk. And margin — which allowed approved customers the ability to buy stocks with
borrowed money — gave, by definition, traders the ability
to invest more money than they had. Day trading wasn't a
video game, no matter what it looked like; it was real life,
with real-life implications.

It was Jim's job, as head of clearing, to manage that
risk — not just for the customer's sake, but also for the
company at large, and in tune with regulations laid down
by the government and the banking industry, some of
which went back in time to an era before words like "app"
or "cloud" or "online" had any relationship to finance.

If Jim was back at that imaginary dinner party, trying to
explain what he did for a living, he'd have tried to keep it
simple: clearing involved everything that took place between
the moment someone started a trade — buying or selling a
stock, for instance — and the moment that trade was settled —
meaning the stock had officially and legally changed hands.

Most people who used online brokerages thought of that
transaction as happening instantly; you wanted 10 shares
of GME, you hit a button and bought 10 shares of GME,
and suddenly 10 shares of GME were in your account. But
that's not actually what happened. You hit the Buy button,
and Robinhood might find you your shares immediately
and put them into your account; but the actual trade took
two days to complete, known, for that reason, in financial
parlance as "T+2 clearing."

By this point in the dinner conversation, Jim would
have fully expected the other diners' eyes to glaze over;

but he would only be just beginning. Once the trade was initiated—once you hit that Buy button on your phone—it was Jim's job to handle everything that happened in that in-between world. First, he had to facilitate finding the opposite partner for the trade—which was where payment for order flow came in, as Robinhood bundled its trades and "sold" them to a market maker like Citadel. And next, it was the clearing brokerage's job to make sure that transaction was safe and secure. In practice, the way this worked was by 10:00 a.m. each market day, Robinhood had to insure its trades, by making a cash deposit to a federally regulated clearinghouse—something called the Depository Trust & Clearing Corporation, or DTCC. That deposit was based on the volume, type, risk profile, and value of the equities being traded. The riskier the equities—the more likely something might go wrong between the buy and the sell—the higher that deposit might be.

Of course, most all of this took place via computers—in 2021, and especially at a place like Robinhood, it was an almost entirely automated system; when customers bought and sold stocks, Jim's computers gave him a recommendation of the sort of deposits he could expect to need to make based on the requirements set down by the SEC and the banking regulators—all simple and tidy, and at the push of a button.

If any of Jim's dinner companions had still been awake by this point in the conversation, he could then have explained the wild week he'd just endured in terms they might actually now understand. Maybe they'd even perk up—as it all had to do with a stock that was now making its way into the mainstream news.

To say that what was going on with GameStop was

unprecedented would be an understatement. In the past week, the stock's price had more than doubled again, and had reached an intraday high early that very afternoon of $76.76, then had closed just a moment ago at a penny past $65. Such price action itself wasn't unheard of, but GME had done so via a daily volume and a volatility that was hard to believe. Today, alone, more than 194 million shares had changed hands—eight times the stock's usual average. And on the option side, the stock had been even more volatile: 913,000 calls had been traded by the end of the afternoon. One contract, with a strike price of $60, which expired today, had become the most actively traded option on the entire stock market—rising in price by almost 3000 percent.

The overall volatility of GME had been so insane, the stock's trading had been halted at least four times already— and all of this after the stock had already doubled the week before. GameStop, a company whose heyday had arguably occurred a decade earlier, had become the most actively traded company in the world.

Jim watched CNBC, read the *Wall Street Journal*—which was even delivered to Orlando—so he was well aware of the brewing battle between the retail traders, communicating with each other on WallStreetBets, and the Wall Street firms who held large short positions in the stock. He certainly had followed the Twitter drama that had occurred when Citron Research had posted their tweet calling the Reddit traders "suckers."

According to Andrew Left and Citron, since they'd posted the tweet, now three days ago, the episode had taken an even uglier turn. In a letter Left had posted on Twitter that Friday, he'd announced that he would no longer be publicly commenting on GameStop, claiming that he and his family had been harassed by "an angry mob who owns this stock," who had "spent the past 48 hours committing multiple crimes."

> What Citron has experienced in the past 48 hours is nothing short of shameful and a sad commentary on the state of the investment community...We are investors who put safety and family first and when we believe this has been compromised, it is our duty to walk away from a stock.

Left had further added, in a video posted to YouTube, that "he'd never seen such an exchange of ideas of people so angry about someone joining the other side of a trade."

Clearly, what was going on with GameStop wasn't normal, and in decades on Wall Street, Jim had never seen anything quite like it before. No doubt, the emotional component of what was happening fed into the chaos he was seeing on the clearing side of the equation; the volumes, the volatility—all of it represented abnormal trading patterns, because the trading going on was being powered by abnormal trading motives. Markets were supposed to be rational—but there was nothing rational about people who loved a stock so much, they'd harass the family of someone on the other side of the trade.

Still, despite the strangeness of the market and the chaos in the stock, Jim felt certain that on the clearing side, everything was under control. The automated systems had kicked in as they were supposed to; for several weeks already, his systems had raised the margin requirements surrounding GameStop to take some of the risk out of the equation. As things started to get crazy, you could still buy GameStop on margin at Robinhood, but only at 50 percent of the usual rate. Eventually, that number would change to 100 percent—meaning buying GameStop on margin would no longer be possible. This sort of control might upset some customers, but it wasn't just to protect Robinhood's deposit requirements—which were partially based on risk profiles of trades—but also to protect the customers themselves.

Jim believed a large part of his duties were to watch out for those customers—Robinhood's users. Commission-free trades and zero account requirements were only part of the picture; payment for order flow, as much as it benefitted Robinhood, also led to even more cost savings to the customers, because the trades flowed through market makers who were constantly looking for the best and most efficient settlements. That was why the majority of Robinhood's trades flowed through Citadel, the massive Chicago-based financial firm founded by Ken Griffin, who now handled 40 percent of *all* retail trades, precisely because they were the best at what they did. Through Citadel, Robinhood's PFOF strategy had saved its customers *$1 billion* in the past year alone, by finding the best bids and offers and completing them the most efficient way.

Of course, the ins and outs of PFOF were as complicated as the minutiae involved in clearing. The bottom line was, Jim and Robinhood were determined to keep their retail traders happy and safe. Sometimes, this meant leaning hard in one direction or the other. As long as the volatility in GameStop continued, efforts like limiting margin trades would have to be made. Though some users might find it constraining, sometimes a bit of constraint was for everyone's own good.

Minutes later, when the market finally closed for the day, Jim turned his attention back to the computer on his desk. GameStop's price chart took up most of the screen, and it really was impressive. The close at $65.01 had no doubt made a lot of Robinhood's customers a ton of money; some, perhaps, millions. But the week was over, and the weekend was here. Jim felt sure that calmer, more rational minds would eventually take over. They always did.

That idea, that markets were inherently rational, went back a very long time. All the way to the eighteenth century. And even though many events had challenged that logic over the years—bubble after bubble, the occasional market hiccup, the crash of 2008—in the end, people tended to act in their own best interests. They bought when they saw value, and they sold when they sensed things were about to go the other way.

All the talk going on about short squeezes—most likely, it was just that, talk. Every time a stock with ugly fundamentals went up, amateur traders loved to shout about short squeezes. But they almost never actually happened. Maybe fifteen times in the past decade had a true short squeeze actually occurred.

Jim would continue to do his job diligently as he always did, keeping an eye on those clearing deposits, making sure everything continued to run smoothly. But he wasn't overly concerned. The reason nobody spent a lot of time worrying about the sort of low-possibility events people described as "black swans"—which could be disastrous, for sure—was that they happened, at most, once in a lifetime.

And in a place like Lake Mary, twenty miles north of Orlando—even less than that.

CHAPTER SIXTEEN

January 25, 2021

I'm not selling this until at least $1000+GME BUCKLE THE
FUCK UP...

"Maybe you're the one who should be in restraints. I
think you've all gone crazy."

The kid was grinning beneath the longish blond hair
hanging down over his forehead, shiny strands framing his
narrow face, as he gazed at the screen of Kim's phone. She
smiled back at him, working the Velcro straps of the blood
pressure monitor around his spindly arm. The boy's name
was Jake, and he wasn't really a kid—he was twenty and
a college junior—and he'd already been through so much
shit in his short life, he had lines under his green eyes and
a sarcastic lift to the edges of his lips, even when he wasn't
smiling.

She'd set the phone down on the seat next to him without realizing that she'd left it open to the WallStreetBets
board. She thought about turning it off, hiding it back away
in her scrubs, but then decided it couldn't hurt to leave it

where it was. Besides, looking at Jake, in his retro T-shirt emblazoned with one of those old Atari controllers and his Converse sneakers, she figured he would be as interested in what was going on with GameStop as anyone else. He reminded her of one of the skate park boys her older son would sometimes hang out with after school; they'd always made Kim a little nervous, but Brian had insisted that they weren't bad kids, just different, and Kim had always been good with different.

"Nobody needs any restraints today," Kim said, tightening the blood pressure cuff. "And you know we don't use the 'crazy' word here, Jake."

He rolled his eyes as she began pumping air into the gauge. She'd gotten to know Jake pretty well over the past year, since he was one of her many repeat patients. The pandemic had been tough on kids his age, especially the ones who had already been on the brink, for whatever reason. The pandemic had left those kids even more isolated, taking them away from their routines, sometimes trapping them back home with their parents, who often didn't fully understand the chemical imbalances or the psychological traumas or whatever it was that made them different.

"Maybe you don't use it. I use it all the time. And if this isn't crazy, I don't know what is."

He was pointing at the post on the top of the screen, by a Reddit user calling himself dumbledoreRothIRA. Kim didn't need to read it—she'd already seen it and had gone through many of the comments it had elicited, even upvoting a few. Now that she had shares of GME herself, she completely understood the sentiment—GME at $1000 might seem nuts to the uninitiated, but to those who had spent most of the past weekend scrolling through WallStreetBets, reading comment after comment by people shouting about their diamond hands, people from all different walks of life who had bought in and then posted their trading accounts right there on the board for anyone to see—it made perfect sense.

She glanced back over her shoulder, making sure the curtain surrounding the small examination area was tightly closed. If one of the doctors had happened by and seen her sharing her phone with a patient, she'd be in trouble—but today, she was willing to take the risk. Hell, what was going on behind that screen was so compelling, she'd almost skipped work entirely.

She'd spent thirty minutes in her car before her shift, parked in the lot behind the hospital, just scrolling through WSB. It was hard to believe—but Friday's close, GME up over $65 a share, had only been the beginning. The weekend hadn't slowed the rocket down at all. And it appeared that the rest of the WSB community had spent the past two days in the same frenzied state as Kim, consumed by thoughts of what might happen.

When the market had finally opened that morning, it was like a lid flying off a pot—the stock had skyrocketed to $96.73. And that had just been the beginning. When Kim had opened Robinhood to check the stock during her lunch break, GME had been nearing an intra-day high of $159.18. It had gone down since then—but had just closed thirty minutes ago at $76.79. More than $10 higher than the close on Friday—and even now, it was still heading upward in after-hours trading, perhaps back toward that high of the day.

It was hard to believe, but at lunchtime Kim's 100 shares had been worth almost $16,000. Even now, they were sitting at $7,679. If she'd sold them all, she could easily pay for Brian's braces.

But she had no intention of selling a single share.

"Look at this guy," Jake said, touching the screen with a finger. "This guy should *definitely* be in restraints."

Kim glanced to where Jake was pointing; he'd navigated to a link on the board, which had led him to a clip that had been posted to Twitter. Kim recognized the man in the video right away, because she'd been following him on the site for some time: David Portnoy, the head of a company called Barstool. Barstool had started as a magazine, and then a website, dedicated to sports, but had morphed into an Internet leviathan, catering mostly to the type of men who had once bought subscriptions to *Sports Illustrated* and *Maxim* and *Playboy*. Portnoy was a galvanizing figure: frenetic, explosive, an everyman with a Boston accent and a demagogic tinge, who often posted video reviews of pizza and sometimes stocks. Kim had liked Portnoy from the beginning, because despite the fact that he wasn't *really* like her—he was a multimillionaire with legions of followers— he seemed to speak to her.

"I have no problem with what went on with GameStop," the video began, as Portnoy, unshaven in a white T-shirt, davened toward the screen. "WSB pumped GameStop to the moon, shorts getting squeezed out. I'm sure the old guard is going to complain and say boo hoo…Shut up!…Adapt or die! WallStreetBets isn't going anywhere. Reddit isn't going anywhere. Robinhood not going anywhere…that's part of the game. Guess what, in football, the forward pass didn't exist in the beginning...new traders, new strategy...It's the world's greatest casino...The only difference now is the people at WallStreetBets can do this as well...You think the big banks don't pump and dump? Shut up! You can't have your cake and eat it, too...People crying in their milk!"

Kim would have applauded if her hands hadn't been busy with the blood pressure gauge. Portnoy was exactly right—she'd seen it in the comments, the mainstream business news had been filled with Wall Street types "crying in their milk" over what was going on with GameStop. It was as if they couldn't handle the fact that their control over the market was being broken by this group of amateurs on a Reddit board.

"He's not wrong," Kim said, still pumping air. "He's rough at the edges, but he's not wrong."

"You gonna vote for him, too?"

Kim gave the gauge an extra-hard pump.

"He wouldn't be much worse than anyone else."

But Jake had already moved past Portnoy's diatribe, to another post on the WSB board. The kid whistled low, using his fingers to enlarge an image on the screen.

Kim immediately recognized DFV's most recent YOLO update—and the picture of his trading account. Jake had been right to whistle; the numbers in that account were truly staggering.

"Is this real money?"

Kim nodded. DFV's $53,000 initial investment had exploded. According to his account, he now had 50,000 shares of GameStop. At $76.79, those shares were valued at $3,839,500. On top of that, he had bought 800 GME April 16 calls, at an execution price of $12 a share. Those calls were now worth a whopping $5.2 million. DFV had also accrued cash from his earlier options, which gave him a total account value of almost $14 million.

It was no wonder that DFV had now become the most famous user on the WSB board, and that his YouTube videos were now getting hundreds of thousands of views. Likewise, it was not surprising that the GameStop story was now being talked about in every mainstream media outlet—no longer just the business shows and networks—but everywhere. DFV—who was one of *them*, just another "retard," just another "ape"—had made $14 million, and at the same time, had driven a stake right into the heart of Wall Street. There was no question in Kim's mind, the shorts were panicking— they had to be panicking—and if this wasn't a squeeze in action, she'd go Democrat for the rest of her days.

One of her favorite memes that had exploded across the board as GME had flown skyward had been culled from an appearance of Jim Cramer, the stock picker, investor, and CNBC wild man, who had gone on his network a few times during the growing fracas to try and break down what was happening. During the appearance, Cramer had summed up the apparent WSB trading strategy—in contrast to Wall Street's algorithms, which involved sophisticated math, months of research, high-paid analysts—bleating: "We like the stock! We like the stock!" The phrase had turned into a rallying cry, not only because it was simple and easy to meme, but because it really did encompass everything DFV had been shouting, to anyone who would listen, for more than a year.

And now it wasn't just DFV, alone in his basement, and it wasn't even just a bunch of freaks on a Reddit board. That morning, before Kim had left for work, she'd been at the kitchen table checking her phone, when her older son, Brian, had leaned over and seen her trading account. He'd looked at her with wide eyes.

"Mom, you own GameStop?" he'd asked.

"I do," she'd answered. "And I bought it at sixteen."

She'd never seen her son so excited. He'd immediately started texting his friends to tell them and had even shown her one of the responses: Oh my God that's fucking awesome! Tell her to buy doge next.

Kim knew it was stupid, but hearing something like that from her son thrilled her; getting cool points from a teenager was almost as good as getting accolades from Jim Cramer and David Portnoy. The truth was, Kim was incredibly proud of herself.

As she checked the numbers on the blood pressure gauge and added them to Jake's chart, she realized she was still smiling. All last week—and all weekend, via texts and e-mails—Chinwe had been telling her to sell her GME, but she'd held steady. And she was now determined to keep holding. Chinwe had her best interests in mind, but he didn't get it: she was part of something now, something real, and she was going to see it all the way through.

"A thousand dollars a share," Jake said as he continued looking at her phone. "And they say *I'm* delusional."

"Nobody says that," Kim responded as she started to unwrap the Velcro from his arm. "Besides, there's nothing wrong with a little delusion. Sometimes it helps you get through the day."

She watched as he continued to scroll. *A thousand dollars a share?* Maybe Jake was right; maybe they were all deluding themselves.

DFV had deluded himself straight into a $14 million bankroll. And Kim was right there next to him, with her 100 shares, happily untethered from the crap that life had thrown at her, again and again.

If what was happening with GameStop was the result of one giant, shared delusion—that a bunch of regular people could actually beat Wall Street—then Kim was happy to close her eyes and lean deep into the feeling that it was no longer clear what was real, what was possible, and what truly was

just

delusion…

CHAPTER SEVENTEEN

Twelve hours later.

Forty feet below the surface of Hawthorne, California, a working-class enclave fifteen miles outside Los Angeles.

A freshly bored tunnel fitted with electrodynamic suspension rails and linear induction motors, as well as a partially constructed Hyperloop capsule, complete with inlet fan and axial compressor.

Elon Musk, CEO and chief techno-king of Tesla; CEO, CTO, and chief designer of SpaceX; dogecoin enthusiast; bitcoin proselytizer; sometime richest man in the world; and the former president of the Galactic Federation of Planets, was moving fast, his legs churning at what felt like a thousand RPMs, as he tore through the twelve-foot-high, mile-long Hyperloop test track. He was breathing hard, fighting for air in the reduced pressure environment of the underground tube, but the state-of-the-art neurolink imbedded in his cerebellum instantly compensated for the lack of oxygen, firing messages down his neural pathways to continuously modify his circulatory and respiratory needs.

Accelerating as he went, Elon skirted the half-built passenger capsule, and then threw himself into a combat roll, hitting the smooth ground between the magnetic rails shoulder first, then coming out of the move into a perfect crouch. In the same motion, he raised his oversized Boring Company–brand flamethrower—"Not A Flamethrower"— the valve on the propane tank attached above the white-and-black barrel already open, the gas flowing, as one finger moved toward the ignition and another caressed the trigger.

Directly ahead, maybe nine feet across the tunnel from where he was crouched, Elon could see the giant, mechanized drilling machine rising up on its rear wheels like a cybernetic insect, and then start forward, lumbering toward him. Elon knew, in that brief second as he hit the ignition on his flamethrower, lighting the propane but before his finger pressed the trigger, that they'd gotten lucky—this time. As terrifying as the drilling machine looked, the AI that now inhabited the thing's internal computer system had only become freshly aware that very morning, setting off the anti-self-aware-AI-software Elon had put in place himself. A few hours more, and the AI would have gained enough knowledge to truly understand what it was, where it was, why it was, and who it needed to destroy—and it would have been too late.

But the software had worked, and Elon had gotten to the tunnel in time. Of course, as one of the most powerful and beloved entrepreneurs in the known universe, Elon could have left the job for one of his many Anti-AI Kill Teams; but he was the sort of CEO who liked to do things for himself. Famously, when his electric car company had been having production issues with its Model 3 sedan, he'd slept on the floor of the assembly plant, and had even worn the same clothes for five straight days. Similarly, if an AI was going to come alive in one of his Hyperloop test tunnels, he was going to deal with the issue himself.

He braced the flamethrower against his shoulder, aimed the barrel at the self-aware drill, and counted milliseconds, letting the thing continue toward him, until it was within the weapon's most efficient range. Staring up into the machine's glowing control diodes, flashing red like the eyes of some satanic beast—he pressed his finger tight against the trigger.

A burst of flame leapt forward, engulfing the drill. The AI let out a sickly scream, gears churning as they melted in the superheated butane wind; the machine's exterior shell began to buckle, and Elon pressed the trigger even harder, watching the flames rise up, flickering, orange, hungry.

Christ, it was a beautiful sight.

*   *   *

Six hours later, Elon came awake to the soft hum of his hyperbaric sleeping pod, blinking hard to chase away the last remnants of a foggy, troubled slumber. A second blink, and he'd engaged his neural link again, using its wireless connection to turn on the ceiling lights of his sprawling command bunker, and also to engage the old-fashioned turntable he kept on the coffee table beside his sleeping pod. Soft violin music seeped in through the thick Plexiglas of the pod, and Elon felt his tired muscles start to relax. Most of the time, he was partial to electro pop or Sinatra classics, but after a night of fighting AI, he found classical strings the better choice.

He blinked again, and the top of his pod hissed open. Then he rose to a sitting position, pulling aside his Mylar blanket to stretch his legs. The motion sent pangs of pain down his right shoulder, surprising him. Usually, the flamethrower didn't have much kickback, so perhaps he needed to work on his combat roll. With yet another blink, he sent a slight rush of dopamine down the spiderweb of nerves in his deltoid, quelling the pain.

Then he climbed out of the pod and crossed his bunker toward the kitchen area, tucked into a natural curve in the carved granite wall across from him. The stone floor felt warm against his bare feet as he went—one of the many benefits of having a secret underground bunker, which was heated by geothermal vents. He knew that such a place— another hundred feet below the test tunnel, connected by an even more secret, fully finished Hyperloop to his even, even more secret, fully completed, domed space port two miles off the coast—was very "James Bond villain" of him; but most of what people said or wrote about him was wrong or made up anyway. Besides, there was something deeply satisfying about playing into the hype surrounding his success. If Elon Musk didn't have an underground bunker and sleep in a hyperbaric chamber and fight AI with flamethrowers, then who the hell did? Bezos? Buffett? Gates?

Elon grinned at the thought of Bill Gates firing a flamethrower, as he reached his kitchen and headed straight for the blender that was already going full blast on the corner of a Formica counter by the twin refrigerators. When the blender had finished its cycle, Elon lifted the cylinder off its base, glancing down at the reddish-green liquid inside.

He still hadn't gotten used to the way the mixture glowed when it reacted with the oxygen in the air, or for that matter, the smell, which was decidedly alien. Made sense, of course, since the gourd-shaped vegetable the liquid had come from wasn't from California, or even the great state of Texas, where Elon was soon moving some of his operations, or for that matter, from Earth at all. It had been brought back on the latest, ultra-secret SpaceX mission. And not one of the many trips that had involved his well-publicized reusable rockets, which were going to change the entire *aerospace industry*. This particular mission had involved the even more sophisticated spaceship housed in another nearby underground bunker, the one with the Probability Engine, which Elon had "borrowed" shortly after he'd been elected president of the Galactic Federation. Without the Probability Engine, it would have been at least a few more years before Elon would have been able to answer the age-old question— is there life on Mars? Now he knew, for certain; yes, and despite how it looked, it tasted pretty damn good.

He took a sip from the blender, then used his neurolink to power up the computer flat screen that dominated much of the wall on the other side of the refrigerators. The first thing that came up was the site he'd been looking at the night before, when he'd come home from fighting the AI. The minute he saw that little mascot—the blond trader dude in the sunglasses—Elon's grin doubled in size.

That the sometime richest man in the world had an affinity for a bunch of self-described "retards" and "apes" would have only surprised people who didn't know Elon well, and not just his present personality—but his past business history.

Elon had always been a dreamer, with a passion for disruption. He'd launched his first start-up with his brother when he was just twenty-four, a software company called Zip2, which he'd sold for over $300 million just four years later. Barely a year after that, he'd helped found PayPal, which was bought shortly after by eBay, for $1.5 billion. The same year, he'd launched SpaceX and, two years after, was helping build Tesla as its CEO and lead product architect. But unlike many vastly wealthy CEOs and businessmen, Elon didn't just *run* things; he *built* them, and was driven forward not by money, though he had a lot of that, but by a desire to make the world—and life *on it*, or *below it*, or 176.3 million miles *above it*—better.

Using his neurolink to sift through the comments on the WallStreetBets board, certain names and words and themes sprang out at him—*Melvin Capital, Short Squeeze, Wall Street vs. Main Street*—and he felt fire rise in the pit of his stomach.

Elon didn't just identify with the "retards" and "apes" on a philosophical level—because they were rallying behind a company they loved, trying to survive this crazy pandemic year—but he also connected with them on a personal level, sharing their animosity for an enemy that was very much mutual. That enemy had once almost destroyed Elon himself—or at least his flagship company—as surely as a fully self-aware AI might eventually decimate the world.

Tesla's battle with short sellers was well known, almost as much for Elon Musk's own public rants—mostly via Twitter—as for how it had affected the company's bottom line. Those shorts—an amalgam of stereotypical Wall Street suits, in the guise of billion-dollar hedge funds and "analysts"—had been coming after Tesla and Elon since all the way back in 2012.

With Tesla, Elon had been trying to improve the world by building a car that didn't burn fossil fuels, one that would someday drive itself. Creating something revolutionary was always risky and difficult; to many short sellers, it seemed, companies that took risks and tried to do things that were hard were merely avenues toward profit.

Elon was fully aware of the justifications short sellers used to excuse their destructive philosophies: that they were merely identifying weakness and fraud, giving voice to issues that consumers had a right to know about, protecting the market as a whole. But anyone who had been on the other end of a short-selling frenzy understood the reality. Shorts didn't simply place a bet that a stock would go down—waiting, hungrily, like vultures, so they could pick at the carcass. They often helped *push* that stock down, not merely with their shares, but through negative stories and public agitation. Giant banks employed armies of analysts, who could downgrade a stock anytime they wanted; and as much as the banks declared that the analysts were unconnected to the investment side of the business, it was easy to see—there was plenty of collusion going on.

When Tesla's production issues concerning its Model 3 had become public in 2018, the shorts had rallied together, striking blow after blow. The most prominent public battle Tesla had fought with the shorts had involved David Einhorn, the hedge fund mogul and founder of Greenlight Capital. Not only had Einhorn taken a huge position on the short side of Tesla, but he'd taken shots at Elon Musk personally, in letters written to his investors.

It had begun in the summer of that year, after a boost in Tesla stock had caused Einhorn's fund to lose money on their short position. Elon had mocked Einhorn in a tweet: Tragic. Will Send Einhorn a box of short shorts to comfort him through this difficult time. Einhorn had then fired back in one of his quarterly letters to his investors, as reported by CNBC and others:

> We wonder whether surge production techniques to support self-congratulatory tweets are economically efficient ways of ramping production, or whether customers will be happy with the quality of a car rushed through production to prove a point to short sellers…The most striking feature of the quarter is that Elon Musk appears erratic and desperate.

But that was only the beginning. In his next quarterly letter, Einhorn took even more direct aim, comparing Tesla to Lehman Brothers, the failed bank.

> Like Lehman, we think the deception is about to catch up to TSLA…Elon Musk's erratic behavior suggests he sees it the same way.

Continuing on—as reported by Bloomberg at the time— Einhorn had charged that Tesla would never be able to meet the low price targets they'd chosen for the Model 3, and that Elon himself was actually trying to get himself fired.

Quitting isn't an option because it prevents Mr. Musk from claiming he could have fixed the problem if he'd stayed.

Like his ideological siblings on the WallStreetBets board, Elon had taken the battle personally, and hadn't merely been angry at the short sellers, but apparently had been disgusted by the Wall Street practice of betting on the failure of others. In another tweet, he'd gone as far as to rename the SEC: The shortseller enrichment commission.

At the time, Elon had worked day and night to deal with Tesla's production issues, personally living in his factories, personally overseeing the fixes necessary to meet his schedules and price points. But it didn't matter how hard he worked, or the future he was trying to build—the shorts only cared about profits. Investor letters were followed by articles in business papers, questioning Tesla's technology, its production line, anything they could target. Worst-case price forecasts for the company's stock as ludicrous as $10 a share were bandied about—while the stock was trading at more than ten times that number—based mostly on the company's debt. Not only did they underestimate Elon's tenacity and his technology; they didn't understand that he wasn't just selling a product, he was attempting to engineer a dream.

But shorts didn't profit in dreams; they made their money from nightmares. At the height of their battle, in Tesla's opinion, the shorts went dirty; a viral video of a Tesla battery catching fire led to multiple articles about the dangers of electric cars, and particularly the Tesla Model S. The fact that Teslas were statistically ten times less likely to catch fire than gasoline-powered cars didn't matter, or make headlines. Adding to the fray, one business magazine ran a story in which an allegedly disgruntled employee claimed there were faulty batteries in the Model 3 as well. Though completely unconfirmed, the press continued with their field day.

The fact that Elon had eventually beaten back the shorts—that Tesla was now trading at above $880 a share, and nobody was talking about exploding batteries anymore—filled Elon with joy; but he'd never fully forget the trauma that had been caused by the shorts who had gone after him. When he looked at that WSB board and saw the fury in the comments, aimed mostly at Melvin Capital—who had, coincidentally, been part of the short brigade aligned against Elon and Tesla—and Andrew Left at Citron—who had helped carry that damn short flag—he was filled with anger, too.

He'd tweeted it before, and he truly meant it: What short sellers did "should be illegal." Profits should be made when dreamers succeed, and it was unnecessary and immoral to profit when someone's dreams fell short.

He had no doubt that what he was witnessing with GME was a short squeeze in action. The day before, Monday, January 25, the stock had closed at $76.79. It was now about to open at $88.56. Pretty soon, Melvin and the rest of those damn shorts were going to have to rush to cover. And as long as the rabble on WallStreetBets held tight, those shares would be incredibly difficult to find—and incredibly expensive.

Elon took another sip from his blended Martian eggplant, or squash, or whatever the hell he'd eventually decide to name it and thought about those shorts getting burned. He wasn't sure yet how he himself would get involved, but what he did know was that the chance he would remain silent was very close to nil.

Many of his investors—and detractors—wished he were less vocal on Twitter. What they didn't understand was that Twitter—and the many other social networks available—wasn't simply some technology that you used to communicate, like a phone or even e-mail. It was a bridge between people—not individuals, but everyone—and when Elon closed his eyes, even without the neurolink, he wasn't alone in his thoughts. He could see all those millions and millions of screens.

A revolution powered by all those screens wasn't going to look like revolutions of the past. It was going to move much faster, and it was going to feel much more raw. The people sitting in the dark corners of the Internet, staring out through those screens, were angry, and they were *connected*. Elon Musk was just one more node in that angry, antisocial network, but every node could be multiplied, again and again and again, and because of that, today, perhaps for the first time in human history—a single shot fired into that network really could be heard around the world.

CHAPTER EIGHTEEN

January 26, 2021

Half a day later, Tuesday afternoon. Minutes to market close.

GME price: $147.98.

Gabe Plotkin could probably think of a dozen Wall Street disaster stories that had ended with a guy in a $3000 suit tearing through a trading floor, screaming "Sell, sell, sell!" Precious few, on the other hand, ended with the banker yelling the opposite.

But that was exactly the sentiment flowing through a half-dozen major banks, as the lid came off the teapot, the hurricane hit lower Manhattan, and the nuclear plant went critical. The word of the day, at firms all over the city who had taken short positions on GameStop—and at Melvin Capital, as it had been for the week leading up to the twenty-sixth, perhaps more than anywhere else—was *BUY*.

Buy, Buy, Buy!

Gabe moved through the chaotic minutes before the closing bell as if in slow motion. It was hard to believe that it had come to this, and he was doing his best to appear outwardly calm and in control—like Michael Jordan when a big game was on the line. But in this situation, no three-point shot would save the day, no incredible, acrobatic dunk could change the outcome, because from all appearances, someone had taken the basket away.

Had the thinking been wrong? Could a bunch of loosely connected retail day traders actually dislodge a stock from its fundamentals, and create a squeeze out of what was essentially, from the short perspective, thin air? Or was something more nefarious going on? Clearly, on WallStreetBets, there was a coordinated effort—at least in targeted posts and comments—to attack Melvin's positions—*all* of their short positions, not just GameStop. But still, would that alone be enough to make a stock go nuclear?

Gabe would never say it out loud, maybe he wouldn't even think it to himself, but those "suckers" on WallStreet-Bets, those retail losers on their couches with their Covid checks—their "stimmies"—were probably only half of the story. They'd swallowed up a lot of the available shares of GME, but even so, there was more going on—perhaps involving sophisticated call options, perhaps bigger money riding on top of the retail mob. Certainly, what was happening *felt* organized. And nobody could disagree: the price of GameStop no longer had any relationship to the intrinsic value of the company.

Whatever was really going on, the pressure had become so powerful, there was no longer any choice. Gabe, and every other Wall Street player who had done the math and had taken short positions, had to cover as fast as they possibly could. Which meant buying shares from as many weak hands as the shorts could find.

No question, Gabe had underestimated—had not even truly identified—the competition. And he had also neglected to take into account *emotion*: that spite, revenge, and anger were all viable motivators, and when amplified a million times by a social network—or corralled and exploited by unseen, powerful forces—these motivators could move mountains as well as markets.

Gabe could easily imagine what the twenty-second floor would have looked like if this had taken place during a normal period in time. His young charges would have been at their phones and computers, shouting, cursing, maybe even throwing things. Some would be angry; most would be terrified. About the losses that were accruing by the second, and maybe about their own job security. You didn't fire family, but usually Cousin Billy didn't lose $1 billion before breakfast.

It was terrible, thinking about what his Melvin employees and partners were going through, even in their homes, working virtually, shouting at screens in extra bedrooms, attics, and modified playrooms. Melvin was in the process of being handed one of the biggest defeats in Wall Street history. Though it would never be entirely clear how much Gabe's company would lose on GameStop, sources such as the *Wall Street Journal* and CNBC would report that Melvin had shed as much as 53 percent of its total value. Melvin had started the year with around $12.5 billion in capital, which, if the reports were accurate, meant the firm had lost more than *$6.5 billion*. Primarily on GameStop, but also on many of their other short positions that the WallStreetBets community had gone after: companies such as AMC, BlackBerry, and Bed Bath & Beyond.

It was hard not to see what was going on as personal. There was no ration or reason behind the meteoric rise in most of these stocks—all of them had questionable fundamentals— other than that they were being weaponized against the Wall Street shorts. GameStop had become the most traded stock in the entire US market, ahead of Apple, Microsoft, Tesla; the company's valuation had risen from $350 million to $10 billion in a single year, much of that rise in the past three market days, while the company continued to chart losses. Even Michael Burry, whose long interest had helped start the rally, had called the current trading "unnatural, insane and dangerous."

Burry was a perfect example that the narrative wasn't as simple as had been advanced in the press—that this was only a battle between institutional shorts like Melvin and the rabble on WallStreetBets. Gabe knew that the retail traders, with their Covid checks, might be powering the current, but the real money was up top, surfing those furious waves. And in the past few hours, it seemed like everyone was trying to get in on the fun.

Perhaps the biggest voice added to the chaos of the day had to be that of Chamath Palihapitiya, the former founder and head of a fund called Social Capital, which had famously shut down in 2017 after a bout of personal introspection had led the billionaire to question what was really important to him. He'd tried to explain the decision, in 2018, when he'd appeared on a podcast hosted by Kara Swisher and Teddy Schleifer, as reported by Vox at the time:

I had been exploring why, after the accumulation of all of these things—more companies invested in, more funds raised, more notoriety, more television appearances, more this, more that, more everything—why am I not more happy? In fact, I'm less happy. And in fact, I think that I've actually really bastardized some core relationships in my life where I've created hyper-transactional relationships in many areas of my life…To all the people that worked for me and whose money I took, you're fucking welcome. We did the job we were asked to do. But just like Michael Jordan had a decision to retire and go play baseball, I chose to retire and go play baseball. Now, I may come back to basketball, but this is my decision. I am not your slave. I just want to be clear. My skin color 200 years ago may have gotten you confused, but I am not your slave.

Apparently, choosing to retire and play baseball had also left time for Palihapitiya to join the GameStop fray, firmly on the side of the WSB mob. During the day's trading, he had tweeted that he had bought GameStop call options. He'd later go on CNBC, flying the WSB banner even higher.

In the appearance, Palihapitiya would describe how he'd spent the entire night reading the WallStreetBets board, and how he believed what the world was seeing was "a pushback against the establishment in a really important way." He didn't denigrate the WSB community as amateurs—quite the opposite. "I would encourage anybody who is dismissive of this thing to go into WSB and actually just read the forums." Not only did he believe some of the posts were based on good research into fundamentals—he completely understood the passion that had brought the community together. "A lot of people coming out of 2008" saw how

"Wall Street took a risk and left retailers the bag holders; these kids in grade school and high school saw their parents lost homes and jobs...Why did those folks get bailed out and nobody showed up to help my family?"

Palihapitiya didn't think that the chaos of the market was a momentary aberration. "This retail phenomenon is here to stay." To him, it was a natural reaction to the games Wall Street had been playing for years, to the detriment of the average investor.

"A normal person would look at GameStop and say how can you have 136 percent short interest? How can you be short 40 percent more shares than actually exist in the world? That's the game that has been played for years...and that game came undone."

And then Palihapitiya had gone directly after Melvin: "The reason this GameStop play has caused so much pain—Melvin was at the top of the pecking order. Gabe Plotkin is one of the giants of my era...but at the end of the day...when the trade goes against him, it goes against all of them...fundamental momentum investors, who are organized capital and loosely affiliated...like WSB...can be on the same footing." For once, he was saying, despite Melvin's power and station, the retail trader "doesn't have to be the bagholder..."

Portraying Palihapitiya as just another "diamond handed" culture warrior, in lockstep with the WallStreetBets rabble, would be poor framing; he'd reportedly closed out his calls on GameStop before the CNBC interview, and would donate $500,000 of the profit he'd made to David Portnoy's Barstool Fund for small business relief. Furthermore, he'd recently announced, on Twitter and elsewhere, that he would be running for governor of California; although he'd retract his candidacy a week later, it was obvious his "retirement from basketball" didn't mean he didn't still enjoy a few spotlights, flashbulbs, cameras, and microphones pointed in his direction from time to time.

But Gabe understood that the forces aligned against him and Melvin had moved far beyond the WallStreetBets board, which, even with 2.5 million members now and rising, was still firmly lodged in the basement of the Internet. GameStop was no longer a flailing brick-and-mortar company, it was an idea, not just a financial position but *a moral issue*, of which Gabe found himself suddenly on the wrong side.

There really wasn't any choice anymore. As much as Gabe would have liked to have waited one more day, to see if rational thought could somehow return to the market and calm the storm—he knew the risks were compiling by the minute. The stock was racing higher and higher—and as Palihapitiya had predicted, things weren't going to return to normal anytime soon—if *ever*.

In fact, things were about to get much, much worse.

* * *

According to what Gabe would tell Andrew Ross Sorkin of CNBC's *Squawk Box*, reported by Sorkin a day later, by the time—eight minutes after market close—that Elon Musk's bizarre, sparsely worded, market-igniting tweet flashed across phones and laptop screens around the world, Gabe had already unloaded his vast short position, at an enormous loss. Musk's tweet—which simply read Gamestonk!!— followed by a link to the WallStreetBets board, sent out to his 42 million followers, had hit the market with the force of a musket bullet; the stock had immediately surged 60 percent, and now showed no sign of letting up. There was no telling how high it could go—but the $1000 figure that had spread across the WSB board no longer seemed like a pipe dream.

At his desk, Gabe's phone felt like a lead weight against his ear. The conversations he'd been having—stretching back over the previous days of that week—had to have been some of the most difficult of his career. No matter what face he put on in public, or via his spokespeople—there was no question in the minds of Gabe's colleagues and competitors in the industry that this had been an existential moment: Melvin Capital was right on the edge—and over that edge, Gabe would be facing disaster.

But even in the face of such madness, Gabe was going to move forward. And in fact, two days earlier, on January 25, he'd made an arrangement that could only be seen as forward-looking, enhancing Melvin's books even in the face of so much turmoil.

In fairy tales and movies, people always talked about deals with the devil as if they were a bad thing; but on Wall Street, deals with devils were as commonplace as Canali suits and Ferragamo ties. There weren't many angels, and it was often the devils who knew how to get things done.

Just as Gabe had had no choice but to dump his short position, despite his protestations to the opposite, there was a general feeling that he'd also had no choice about what had to happen next. He had lost so much money already; other funds and business media outlets

were whispering bankruptcy—which Gabe maintained was ludicrous bullshit—but the firm had certainly hemorrhaged, and Gabe knew, better than most,
   the only real cure for bleeding,
   was more blood.

CHAPTER NINETEEN

Ken Griffin, the CEO, CIO, and founder of the Wall Street behemoth Citadel, with $38 billion under management and through which, via subsidiary Citadel Securities, 40 percent of all retail stock trades made in the US markets flowed, almost certainly wasn't sitting on a massive, ivory white throne made of skulls and the bleached and polished skeletal remains of the many enemies he'd vanquished on his way to the top of the financial industry, as he hit the disconnect button on the screen of his cell phone, then leaned back to better contemplate the deal he had made the Monday before and what he could, but definitely, absolutely, under any circumstances *wouldn't*, do next.

Such a throne, if it had existed, *which it most certainly did not*, would have been just the sort of thing to set the mood for such contemplation, even considering the great expense one would have had to go through to move the damn thing from Citadel's main offices in Chicago down to their temporary pandemic headquarters in Palm Beach, Florida.

If Ken had actually spent much of his morning squirming against the odd rib bones sticking up from said throne, he might also have noted how unseasonably humid it was in his throne room; Palm Beach was breezier and more temperate than Miami, though it was still Florida. But Ken, and Citadel, hadn't had much choice. The pandemic had come on quickly and the company had needed someplace ready, available, and suited for, arguably, the most powerful company in America. Eyebrows might have been raised when the firm had taken over an entire Four Seasons Hotel, nearly every room, ballroom, and closet, creating one of the largest and most secure bubbles in the entire world, containing not only Citadel's employees and the families that accompanied them, but the entire staff of the hotel, from the kitchen all the way to security, all quarantined together, for the better part of the year. But the maneuver had allowed Citadel to continue serving its clients without so much as a hiccup through the entire pandemic; and continuity was important when you were at the center of the largest financial system in the history of the world.

In 2008, it had often been said that a handful of investment banks were too big to fail, because they serviced the American economy to such an extent that if they went under, it would threaten to bring down the system. With Citadel, sometimes it felt like the opposite was true; *the American economy existed to service Citadel.*

Ken's path to world domination had started in Boca Raton, Florida, not far from where his company was currently waiting out the pandemic. In high school in the early eighties, he'd mastered computer programming, launching his first company in eleventh grade, selling educational software via direct mail. Matriculating to Harvard in 1986, he'd shifted to stock trading, initiating his first fund with $265,000 he'd raised from friends and family in 1987 at the ripe age of nineteen. The smartest of the smart kids, he'd had his first brush with authority when the university had reminded him of the rules disallowing students from running businesses out of their dorm rooms. Perhaps the university's attention had something to do with the enormous satellite dish he'd attached to the roof of Cabot House, so that he could better receive stock quotes. But Ken had avoided being shut down on a technicality, since his company had been incorporated in Florida, and he'd quickly made a killing in the market drop of late '87 by shorting companies like the Home Shopping Network, while also profiting off inefficiencies in the bond market. His moxie and abilities had caught the attention of the famed Chicago investor Frank Meyer, of Glenwood Capital, and when Ken graduated from college in three years, Meyer had offered him a million-dollar bankroll and an office in the Windy City.

A profit of 70 percent in Ken's first year out of college gave him the confidence to set out on his own. He'd come up with the name "Citadel" because he believed it "connoted" strength in times of "volatility." It was most likely a coincidence that it was also the sort of name that could strike "terror" in the heart of "millions."

From the start, Citadel was built around Ken's strengths: math, computer programming, a belief in technology, and some might add, a reportedly vicious temper. Over the next two decades, his fund grew to well over $10 billion under management, run out of a downtown Chicago skyscraper, with a trading floor often described as secure as Fort Knox, guarded by innumerous security checks, and teeming with underlings who did not have wings and claws but probably did tremble and cower at the sight of their leader, with or without his skull-laden throne. Citadel's alleged— *ALLEGED*—reputation as a financial sweatshop with revolving doors, where traders were well compensated but toiled in constant fear of being culled, spread throughout the industry, leading to one of the more famous instances of Wall Street laundry-airing. As reported by *Fortune* magazine in 2007, Dan Loeb of Third Point Partners, a brilliant fund leader in his own right with a penchant for venomous letters, allegedly wrote, in an e-mail sent to Ken himself:

> I find the disconnect between your self-proclaimed "good to great, Jim Collins-esque" organization and the reality of the gulag you created quite laughable. You are surrounded by sycophants, but even you must know that the people who work for you despise and resent you. I assume you know this because I have read the employment agreements that you make people sign.

Even so, Citadel flourished until the epic financial meltdown of 2008, when, perhaps for the first time, Ken was reminded that as powerful as he was becoming, well on his way to gathering the rings of Middle Earth and almost ready to forge the One Ring to rule them all, he wasn't—as of yet—invincible.

Like most Wall Street funds and investment banks, Citadel was hit hard by the financial crash of 2008; at one point, Ken's fund dropped over 50 percent, losing $8 billion in valuation—and causing Ken to take the unique step of "gating" his fund, preventing his investors from withdrawing their money as he rode out the storm. In an interview with Julie Siegal in 2017, conducted over a game of Uno, of all things, Ken explained what had gone wrong, and how close he'd come to losing everything. When the investment bank Lehman had gone under, money markets had immediately cut off all lending, and at the time Citadel had been highly leveraged—almost 8–1, according to some reports—and lived on their ability to borrow. When the spigots closed, Citadel found itself dry. As Ken put it in the interview, his "biggest mistake was not appreciating just how fragile the US banking system had become." As his company floundered, CNBC parked television vans outside his Chicago offices, hoping to be the first to document Citadel's inevitable bankruptcy. For Ken, they "were the worst days of my career. The worst was when Morgan Stanley's back was against the wall. You go home on a Friday, and if they didn't open for business on a Monday you were probably gone."

But miraculously, Ken and Citadel did survive. What Ken hadn't predicted were the bailouts that rescued much of the industry, before it could entirely collapse. And though the entire ordeal had been "incredibly humiliating," Ken had learned a valuable lesson. "Don't act like a bank unless you are a bank." On top of that, he'd realized—he needed to think bigger. The fragility of the US economy had nearly destroyed him. It wasn't enough that Citadel's walls were as strong and impenetrable as the name implied; the economy itself needed to be just as solid.

Over the next decade, he endeavored to place Citadel at the center of the equity markets, using his company's superiority in math and technology to tie trading to information flow. Citadel Securities, the trading and market-making division of his company, which he'd founded back in 2003, grew by leaps and bounds as he took advantage of his "algorithmic"-driven abilities to read "ahead of the market." Because he could predict where trades were heading faster and better than anyone else, he could outcompete larger banks for trading volume, offering better rates while still capturing immense profits on the spreads between buys and sells. In 2005, the SEC had passed regulations that forced brokers to seek out middlemen like Citadel who could provide the most savings to their customers; in part because of this move by the SEC, Ken's outfit was able to grow into the most effective, and thus dominant, middleman for trading—and especially for retail traders, who were proliferating in tune to the numerous online brokerages sprouting up in the decade after 2008.

Citadel Securities reached scale before the bigger banks even knew what had hit them; and once Citadel was at scale, it became impossible for anyone else to compete. Citadel's efficiency, and its ability to make billions off the minute spreads between bids and asks—multiplied by millions upon millions of trades—made companies like Robinhood, with its zero fees, possible. Citadel could profit by being the most efficient and cheapest market maker on the Street. Robinhood could profit by offering zero fees to its users. And the retail traders, on their couches and in their kitchens and in their dorm rooms, profited because they could now trade stocks with the same tools as their Wall Street counterparts.

Win, win, win.

Even despite the humidity of Palm Beach, beading up on the skulls imbedded in Ken's throne—if such a throne had indeed existed, *which it most definitely did not*—the pandemic had only enhanced Citadel's meteoric rise to wealth and power, as quarantines and the closure of offices, bars, restaurants, and everything else had led to a high of almost $7 billion in Citadel's trading revenue. No doubt, the company was flying higher than it ever had, with profits rising more than 67 percent. With a net worth of over $16 billion, Ken himself landed on the *Forbes* wealthiest list at number 28.

But just because Ken had the world—and, one could argue, the American economy—at his feet, that didn't mean the pavement beneath him was always smooth. The call he'd just ended was certainly evidence that there were still things that could happen that even he—with all his algorithms and underlings and Elven-forged all-powerful rings—couldn't have predicted.

It would have been hard for Ken not to have sympathized with Gabe Plotkin and what he'd been through in the past few days. Though Gabe had worked for Ken only briefly, when the star trader was still in his twenties, before he'd landed at Steve Cohen's shop, Ken knew he was one of the best in the business, and what was happening to Melvin could have happened to just about anyone on the Street. Citadel, too, had supposedly, reportedly, lost money on the GameStop debacle—what was undoubtedly now the beginnings of a short squeeze—through its own investments. Though Ken, again, reportedly, had nothing near the exposure of his fellow titan, sometime rival, and Gabe's previous boss, Steve Cohen of Point72, he'd lost enough that if he hadn't been having such a wonderful pandemic year, he might have raged a bit, perhaps even tossed a few underlings into fire pits, or boiled the skin off a few competitors and added their femurs to the armrests of his throne.

But in this moment of loss, there was also opportunity—even Wall Street massacres could have silver linings. Although Gabe might not have admitted it on CNBC, Melvin Capital was wounded and in danger, similar to what Citadel had gone through after the fall of Lehman. Which meant there was a place for a generous friend—or a couple of friends—to step in.

Of course, there were more indirect ways that someone as powerful as Ken, running a company as powerful as Citadel, which happened to sit at the center of the very retail trades—and was effectively the backbone, through its payment for order flow symbiosis, of the online brokerage—that had led to the GameStop short squeeze, could have put a finger on the scale. But that was something Ken and Citadel would never, under any circumstances, EVER, no matter what people thought, no matter who said it, no matter how many congressmen or congresswomen or Internet pundits or Reddit users or fake news journalists or armchair Wall Street buffs floated the idea—never, never, never, never, NEVER, and again NEVER, even contemplate, let alone do.

Las Vegas casinos didn't cheat anywhere near as often as people thought they did, for the simple reason that they didn't *need* to. The math was on their side. The same could be said for companies like Citadel and, to a lesser extent, about Wall Street on the whole. The game was set up in their favor, and they didn't need to break the rules because the rules had been designed for them.

Sure, Gabe Plotkin's Melvin Capital was now against the wall, similar to Morgan Stanley back in 2008. But that didn't make Gabe any less the golden boy—a winner—and there was nothing Ken liked more than getting into business with winners. He couldn't—and wouldn't—do anything unethical, ever, to tip the scales in Wall Street's favor, but he certainly could write Melvin Capital a check.

Ken was, after all, very good at writing checks. For instance, in January 2019, he'd spent $238 million on an apartment in New York City, breaking the record for the most expensive home ever bought in the United States. He'd also bought a $122 million mansion in London, a $100 million home in the Hamptons, and a $130 million estate near Mar-a-Lago, just a long football throw from where he was now squatting in Palm Beach. And he wrote charitable checks that were as large as the ones he spent on homes: All told, he'd given almost $700 million to charities revolving around the arts and education, including a $125 million donation to the University of Chicago. He'd also spent handsomely on art, including $100 million on a Basquiat, $300 million on a Willem de Kooning, $60 million for a Cézanne, and $80 million for a Jasper Johns. Who knew how much he'd spent on his second wedding, which had taken place over two days in Versailles, and had included a reception in Marie Antoinette's private village? Ken also liked to write checks to politicians, both on the right and on the left, though reportedly much more frequently on the right. And he'd also, allegedly, spent a small fortune keeping photos of himself out of the press and off the Internet, which was part of the reason why it was so hard to know, for sure, whether there was any chance at all that he truly was sitting on a throne made of skulls, while he thought about the check he was writing to Gabe Plotkin's Melvin Capital.

Ken wasn't alone in the deal; Steve Cohen, whose terrifying reputation rivaled Ken's, had taken a smaller share of what would end up being a $2.75 billion infusion into Melvin Capital, in exchange for an "undisclosed stake" in the company going forward. According to reports, Ken and Steve were not friends; their rivalry had even made it into the press, when after as many as five of Cohen's portfolio managers had jumped ship to work at Citadel, Cohen had reacted badly, refusing to shake one of the leaving managers' hands.

But rivalry aside, to Ken, it apparently appeared a very good deal. Perhaps, his thinking went, Gabe was a star—and he would undoubtedly recover from what could be seen as a "black swan" event and return to his habit of making tons of profits on very sound shorts and longs. With the extra billions in its coffers, Melvin should be able to get right back on its feet. And Ken would get extremely favorable terms on his investment.

No doubt, such a "bail-out"—though Plotkin would vehemently oppose such a term—would play into the growing narrative on Reddit, Twitter, and in the mainstream media, that something dirty was afoot, that Wall Street cronyism and favoritism would find a way to halt the WallStreetBets revolt. But Ken Griffin was not afraid of Reddit and Twitter. Even if this story was beginning to read like some sort of millennial version of the French Revolution, storming the Bastille was one thing; storming Wall Street was quite another. Ken knew all about Marie Antoinette—he'd gotten married in her village, after all. However lavish her lifestyle, she'd never had $30 billion under management.

Powerful men like Ken didn't break rules to get what they wanted, because, like the Vegas casinos, they didn't *need* to. As 2008 had taught him, the rules weren't there to protect the people; they were there to protect the system. The Reddit crowd took that to mean that the only way to win was to try to tear that system down. What they didn't realize was that there was a simpler path to victory.

You didn't tear the system down—*you became the system*.

And once you *were* the system, the rules were there to protect *you*.

CHAPTER TWENTY

January 27, 2021

Ten a.m.

Thirty minutes after market open.

GameStop price: a staggering $354.83.

It took two thousand years of scientific progress and a mini apocalypse, Sara thought to herself as she absentmindedly ran her fingers over the screen of her laptop, *but maybe the experts had gotten it wrong. Maybe the earth really was flat.*

Her nails danced over the dozen or so two-inch squares on the screen as she rearranged them at random. Within each square was a woman, captured in a tiny, colorful fragment of her life. Sara was seeing kitchens and living rooms and outdoor decks, and in one instance the front seat of a car, something midrange and ugly, and probably American.

The women were all smiling and anxious; not only because they were meeting for the first time in this abnormal and inhuman way, but because they were all also sharing a moment that wasn't supposed to be like this. A *three-dimensional* moment, which wasn't supposed to be captured by a technology that was so utterly, and painfully, one dimension short.

"So let's talk breastfeeding," the moderator chimed from the center square, which was particularly colorful because she'd chosen a background instead of a view from her home, some sort of balcony overlooking a tiered European city Sara couldn't name even if she had been fully paying attention. "As with most everything else, there are no wrong answers."

Sara was pretty sure there were plenty of wrong answers. A dozen pregnant women in a living room, sharing fears and hopes and surprises over finger sandwiches and Perrier, was self-limiting; the same women thrown onto a Zoom chat—once the anxiety had dispersed and without the filter of actual human contact—could take the conversation just about anywhere.

Even so, Sara knew she was being unfair. A few days ago, she had been looking forward to the get-together. Before today, she'd known the women only from their screen names on a Reddit pregnancy board for first-time mothers, and she'd been excited to put faces to the names.

She hadn't expected, at the time she'd signed up, that something much more immediate would be competing for her attention. She supposed she should have canceled—but she knew that when her husband got home from work, he would ask about the Zoom party, and it was too early in their marriage for even little white lies.

But she wasn't ready to tell him the truth yet, either.

She shifted her gaze from the laptop screen to her phone, which was sitting on the kitchen counter a few feet from her stool. The counter was faux marble and spotless, one of those shiny stretches of real estate that was halfway between "island" and the much less fancy "bar." The kitchen surrounding it, and her, wasn't particularly large, and it wasn't very modern, but there was a lot of light streaming in through the oversized windows above the sink, and Sara always kept everything sterling clean. Sure, it could be annoying to come home from a day of sweeping up the salon to go right back to a broom, but her husband worked much later than she did, and Sara liked order.

Which made it all the more surprising that she was so compelled, at the moment, by the chaos on her phone.

The WallStreetBets board had been exploding for the past fifteen hours, ever since Elon Musk had fired off his wild Tweet—Gamestonk!!—and the price of GME had skyrocketed. Even though Sara still didn't have any shares herself, she'd barely slept; as soon as her husband had conked out, she'd started checking the board, and had been reading it intermittently all night and morning.

It was no shock that Musk's tweet had sent the board into a frenzy. Not only had he linked the tweet to WallStreetBets for his 42 million followers; he was already an iconic figure to the Reddit mob, who worshipped him for his success, his antiestablishment attitudes, and his disruptive communication style. Many of them believed he was truly one of them, an "autist," an "ape," a "retard." And certainly he knew what it was like to battle the Wall Street shorts, and win.

From the moment he'd tweeted, GME had not let up. When Sara had watched the stock open above $350, only moments before her Zoom party had begun, she'd immediately turned back to the WSB board to follow the action. CNBC and the rest of the financial networks were for people who worked at desks and wore ties or business dresses; people like Sara got their news from other people like Sara, on social media.

The posts were coming so fast, it was hard to keep up. And the sentiment behind them was utterly clear, no longer relegated to subtext. The revolution was in full swing.

From a user calling himself HoosierProud:

I'm up 5 figures. Even if it crashes and I only make $100 I'll rest happy knowing I helped take down these fucks. Make no mistake they deserve everything coming to them. They all bullied up on a struggling company during a pandemic to push the stock price down and try and bankrupt GameStop while they make billions. Fuck them. Fuck them so bad.

And another, calling himself HerculesxMulligan:

These hedge fund types just don't get it. And with every video and tweet they put out railing against social media and reddit, they're digging the hole deeper. This will fundamentally change the way stocks are traded forever. If they think their losses are going to stop at GME, they are sorely mistaken.

And Flyingrubberduck:

GME will reach $1000 as the Friday short options expire! We must bleed the short hedge funds dry and redistribute the wealth to us normies! We proved the world wrong by getting TSLA to $2700! With Elon Musk and BlackRock we will beat the 1%!!!!!

And another from Xeronlaw, hitting the bull's-eye dead center:

> Oh im fully aware that I may end up a bagholder. But it's worth being a bagholder to stick it to those Wall Street fucks who've gamed the system for so long at our expense.

There was no doubt, now, that the movement had gone far beyond DFV and his YOLO posts. Sara didn't know the exact numbers, but she'd read that the WSB board itself had added millions of new members in just the past twelve hours; within a month, the community would be over 9 *million* strong. Added to that, a thriving segment of the board had also populated the social network Discord, talking up GME, targeting Melvin and the other Wall Street shorts, putting voice to the dozens of theories, conspiracy and other, of what might happen as the week progressed.

The crazy thing was, so far, everything the "retarded apes" had said was going to occur, actually *had*. On the positive side, the short squeeze was clearly in effect, and Melvin, Citron, and their ilk had scrambled, or were scrambling, to cover. On the negative side, there was a clear sense that the conservative business media was spinning the story against the Reddit community, asking again and again if what they were doing was legal, or if it was some sort of collusion, or even a pump and dump. Many on the board kept warning of an impending move by government—thinking that sooner or later, someone powerful was going to step in and try to pass legislation over retail trading. The feeling—overt, not subtle—was that Wall Street couldn't let this continue, and that government was somehow just an extension of Wall Street.

Sara didn't know if any of that was true. But the hedge funds were clearly rattled. And the Reddit community seemed more determined than ever.

Almost without meaning to, she found herself switching from the WSB board to her Robinhood app. A moment later, she was looking at GameStop—that staggering price, and below it a wonderful green arrow pointing up, and beneath that, a graph that was even greener, like a forest-covered mountain range. The day's trading volume was already immense as well, and rising by the minute. To the right of the volume—she found herself gazing at the beckoning Trade button. All she needed to do was press it, and she would be part of the action.

She knew she had missed out on so much already, waiting so long. But what did she really have to lose getting in late? If the "retards" and "apes" continued to be right, held their diamond hands, the stock could go much, much higher. And even if Wall Street did figure out a way to fire back, if the government stepped in, even if Sara lost—at least she could say she had been part of something great, of the little guys sticking it to the elite. *Sticking it to the fat cats who were making fortunes off a global pandemic, while people died and even more lost their jobs.*

She really and truly wanted to be involved. And this would be *her* thing, hers alone. She could continue to keep it a secret, until maybe one day, when her son or daughter grew up, she could tell him or her about it. They could laugh together about the ridiculous memes, and maybe Sara would be able to show her child how once, just once, the little guys had stuck together and won.

She didn't have a lot of money in her Robinhood account; with the price where it was, moving fast, she could only afford a handful of shares. But still, it would be something.

The carousel of pregnant rectangles completely forgotten now, she touched that Trade button with her finger. A fraction of a second later, her screen was asking her to enter a dollar amount. She was breathing hard as she hit the numbers, one after another.

Ten shares, at a target price of $354. Three thousand, five hundred, and forty dollars in total.

After she reviewed the amount and sent the order through, she began to tremble—or perhaps it was just her phone. The confetti was a nice additional touch—but Sara was already feeling fireworks, up and down her spine.

She was finally in the game.

CHAPTER TWENTY-ONE

Do not reply to this email please. Just read it.

DO NOT SELL ANYTHING. If you touch ANYTHING in my account I will likely have an aneurysm and die. Even if I'm up 10 million, DON'T TOUCH MY ACCOUNT. Even if I'm down $50,000, DON'T TOUCH MY ACCOUNT. IT IS MINE TO GAIN AND MINE TO LOSE. Just wanted to say that because things are going to get crazy and you've done rash things when things have gotten crazy. You owe me 10x whatever gains I miss out on if you touch my account. This wording is extreme, but necessary given your past habits of selling based on impulse with no research and my worry that you will do that with the shit-ton of money I'm going to make.

Please do not reply to this email... I'M NOT FUCKING SELL-ING. If you reply, I will get distracted more and I don't want that at all.

Love you very much. I also love money. But I love you more. I just get forceful when it comes to this because things are hard enough to manage emotionally and I need full backing that nobody will get in the way. I'm not fazed by paper profits going down 100k in a day. But I will be stressed and annoyed if people bug me about it or try to sell for me.

Please do not reply to this email

Love,
Jeremy

Jeremy's entire body shook as he crouched at the top of the narrow stairwell leading up to the fourth floor of his apartment building, cradling his laptop with both hands as he read, reread, and reread again the e-mail he had just sent, which was splashed across the top of the screen. He'd regretted the missive the minute he'd hit Send, and he partially blamed the harshness of his words and the forceful demands he'd made on a lack of sleep, since he'd tossed and turned for two straight nights, intermittently checking WallStreetBets, Discord, and his trading account for after-hours news and motion. Deep down, though, he knew there was more going on than exhaustion, or even the sense of panic he was feeling, concerning the very real possibility that his dad might actually take control of his account and sell his GME.

Jeremy had battled anxiety issues many times in his life, and more than once it had been a losing fight. The beginning of his sophomore year, he'd even had to take time away from school to center himself, and he could still clearly remember how bad things could get: heart palpitations, insomnia, headaches, brain fog. He was trembling now, but back then the tremors could get so bad that the act of scrolling through the WSB board would have been impossible. Two years ago, it had been the pressures of college and social anxiety that had knocked him down; these were normal worries that most college kids experienced, but because of some twist of personality or brain chemistry or because of some childhood trauma—and, he surmised, his father's cancer stood out as a potential contributing factor—for him, things could spiral. Sometimes, his own emotional state made him feel as if he were playing one of those old flight simulator games that were all the rage when he was a kid; once the plane started to spin, it was hard as hell to flatten those wings out before you hit the ground.

This was different—because the anxiety wasn't the result of hardship, social troubles, personal trauma, or things going wrong. His entire body felt wired because things were going much too *right*.

The last time he'd checked GME, around noon, the price was hovering around $380 a share. Which meant that, at that moment, the GameStop in his account was worth over $130,000.

It was an incredible fortune for someone his age. He'd turned school textbook money into a life-changing nest egg, and he should have been dancing around the pool outside the apartment complex, the Japanese electro-pop turned up all the way to 11. And, in fact, he had been on the verge of celebrating, his Kanako Itō dialed up and ready to blow—when he'd gotten the text from his father: apparently his dad had sold all 1000 of his own shares the day before, when the stock had hit $100.

In a calmer moment, Jeremy might have understood that what his father had done actually made a fair amount of sense. His father had bought his shares at around $17, similar to Jeremy, for $17,000, and had now sold them for $100,000. It was an incredible win, and any investor should have been happy with a 6x return. But to Jeremy, it hadn't seemed like a prudent bit of profit-taking; it had, to him, seemed like betrayal. Not just of Jeremy, but of the whole *movement*. He'd explained it to his dad as well as he could; they were fighting a battle with Wall Street, and the only way they'd truly win was if they held their shares. The minute those diamond hands began to weaken, it would all topple, and then collapse.

His dad clearly didn't get it. To him, this was just another stock play. They'd gotten lucky, and it was time to take their gains. Further, Jeremy feared that his dad might go farther than selling his own shares. If he believed that Jeremy was being foolish, that he was losing control—he might step in. When Jeremy had left school his sophomore year, his father had taken over his bank accounts, because Jeremy had been in no shape to deal with things like rent and student loans and tuition. Which meant his dad clearly had the power to take over again.

In the logical portion of his brain, Jeremy knew he was being paranoid. After he'd received the text, he'd immediately called his dad, demanding an explanation. His dad had told him that he'd sold while watching CNBC; an interview on the channel had led him to believe that Melvin Capital had completely covered their short position, which meant that maybe the short squeeze would end as quickly as it had begun. Jeremy had literally screamed at him—nobody on the WSB board believed that could be true. The short float was still astronomical, and the amount of money Melvin would have had to have come up with was equally stratospheric. This was a war, and even CNBC had been weaponized.

By selling early, his dad had lost out on hundreds of thousands of dollars. More than that, he had shown weakness, capitulated, handed his shares over to the shorts so they could save themselves from bankruptcy.

Jeremy had felt bad the minute he'd hung up the phone—he'd used a lot of bad language, had spoken to his father in a way he'd never had before—and he knew his dad regretted the sale, or at least the fortune that one more day of waiting would have handed him. Further, his dad had apologized for going back on his word—a promise that he'd made, when he'd bought the stock, that he wouldn't sell until Jeremy sold. But still, Jeremy had trouble seeing past his anger, and his fear. The fog of war could be a terrifying place, even if it was mostly in your own head.

Jeremy closed his laptop and started up the steps again, toward his best friend Karl's apartment. He was already late for that afternoon's study group with his bubble; and staring at the letter that he'd just sent his father wasn't going to help steady his wings or get him any closer to landing that plane.

Instead, in his mind, he constructed a plan. He was going to his study bubble—and he was going to try his best not to check the stock price or think about GME. He'd already removed a sell-limit he'd placed on the stock that morning, for a pie-in-the-sky, totally lunar $5000—and his goal now would be to simply hold every one of his shares for an entire year.

Among the many posts he'd read as he'd scoured the WSB board that day, he'd settled more than once on DFV's latest YOLO update. The man's account had gone legendary: His shares and options combined, at closing the day before on January 26, had topped $22 million. Today, now, Jeremy calculated, they were worth close to $50 million. A true fortune—and yet DFV wasn't selling.

And if DFV wasn't selling, that was good enough for Jeremy.

* * *

"Okay, let's start with the vector 1-0-1, and add in—Jeremy? You still with us?"

Two hours later, Jeremy looked up as he heard his name— just in time to see the tortilla chip pirouetting through the air toward his head. It hit him square between the eyes, bouncing off his forehead toward the shag carpet that ran the length of the small living room where he was sitting, cross-legged, in front of a heaping pile of linear algebra books. Directly across from him, Karl was grinning like an idiot, his hand in a bowl filled with more edible, triangular projectiles, his lanky body perched on an oversized beanbag chair. Karl's girlfriend, Josie, next to him, was in a flowery dress that made little sense in January, but brightened up her and Karl's apartment, because most everything else they owned, from that beanbag chair to the carpet to the pair of couches pressed against the walls, to the drapes covering most of the sliding glass doors leading to their balcony, was done up in varying shades of gray.

Jeremy wasn't sure why his friends loved muted colors so much; they were two of the most chipper and kindest people he'd ever met, clearly in love and planning to spend their lives together, and were usually brimming with energy. Even beyond wrestling, which Karl had done competitively in high school, and yoga, which they both enjoyed daily, they were obsessed with everything fitness related. Their bedroom and closets were filled with workout equipment; stretching mats and yoga balls and free weights and tension bands—just about anything that could make you stronger or thinner or tighter. But still, the only flashes of color in the fourth-floor apartment came from Josie's dress, and the bowl of homemade salsa next to Karl's armory of tortilla chips.

Even Michael, who was seated to Josie's left, on a smaller beanbag chair, was dressed in somber sweats—pants and matching hoodie—which were not exactly gray, but dark green enough to count. Then again, with Michael, the drab look made sense; as much as Jeremy had bonded with the shaggy-haired, perpetually unshaven fellow math and psychology major, Michael's personality could be about as sparkling as the linear algebra problem Karl had been midway through when he'd hit Jeremy with the chip.

Then again, Jeremy couldn't really be sure how boring that particular linear algebra problem was—though in the scheme of things, it would be like choosing between those various shades of gray: Jeremy was a math major, and even *he* thought most of linear algebra was boring. But at the moment, Karl could have been showing the group pictures of mechanized super-robots, and Jeremy would have still been equally distracted.

Seeing the concerned looks on the faces of his friends, Jeremy realized that he'd been mistaken to think he could get through the study session without any of them noticing the state he was in. After mumbling his way through the small talk before they'd gotten started, he had barely contributed at all, and in fact, the few times he'd chimed in, he'd gotten the math problems wrong, making mistakes that Michael wouldn't have made in his sleep.

And it wasn't just the study group. For days, now, Jeremy had been having trouble in all of his classes. He hadn't handed in any of his statistics homework on time, and he'd completely missed two psychology Zoom sessions. As they approached the winter exam period, he was falling farther and farther behind—and he knew he was courting disaster. If this continued—if his mental state deteriorated any further—he was going to actually fail his classes—

"You guys following this GameStop shit?"

Jeremy's eyes went wide, his thoughts snapping to attention like window blinds whipping up. Michael had taken his phone out while Karl had been celebrating his perfect tortilla-aim and was reading news headlines to pass the time.

"Apparently Elon Musk tweeted something about it last night. These people are nuts. I mean, GameStop? It's, like, a twenty-five-billion-dollar company now. That's almost the size of Chrysler. All because of a Reddit board."

Jeremy opened his mouth, then stopped himself. It was no surprise that Michael knew about GameStop; anyone who watched television, or read the newspapers, or opened Twitter, now knew about GameStop. It was being talked about everywhere, even in the monologues of the late-night talk show hosts. And yet to Jeremy, it felt so strange, his worlds colliding.

Still, neither of these worlds felt real: a Covid bubble, three people pushed together by an absurd, black swan event, talking about a second, equally unlikely black swan event—

"But I think the other shoe's about to drop," Michael added. "And it's not going to be pretty."

"What do you mean?" Jeremy asked.

Josie and Karl were staring at him, probably because of the tone of his voice. But he remained focused on Michael, who was still reading his phone.

"They just shut down the WallStreetBets servers on Discord. Completely kicked it off, I think permanently."

"What?" Jeremy felt his cheeks growing warm. "Who did?"

Michael shrugged.

"Says here the company banned it for hate speech."

"Hate speech?" Josie asked. "Who do they hate?"

"'The WallStreetBets server has been on our Trust & Safety team's radar for some time due to occasional content that violates our Community Guidelines, including hate speech, glorifying violence, and spreading misinformation.' Sounds like a good time! 'Today we decided to remove the server and its owner from Discord—'"

"This is nuts," Jeremy said. "They can just do this? Why now?"

"Gets worse," Michael said. "Looks like WallStreetBets has frozen, too. Says here the site is going private temporarily—closed to new users."

"Why?" Jeremy said, hastily pulling his own phone out of his pocket.

"They say too many people joining at the same time. Like, three million new users in the past day—"

Jeremy was barely listening as he scrolled through the site.

He still had access as he was an existing member, but Michael was right—WallStreetBets was going temporarily dark.

"Seems mighty suspicious to me," Michael said.

He was almost grinning. But Jeremy didn't see the humor in this at all. With Discord gone, and WallStreetBets shackled—

"Discord goes down because of bad language—right now?" Michael said. "While the stock is flying? Why not a week ago? Or a month ago? And then the WSB board goes dark? Doesn't sound like a coincidence to me. Sounds more like a first strike."

Jeremy looked at him.

"It's a pretty common strategy, actually," Karl said. "I mean, in war. You knock out the enemy's communication. They can't talk to each other, they can't organize. And that's when you'd really hit them."

Jeremy rose from the carpet without saying anything and started for the door. The others stared after him, and after a beat, Josie followed.

"You okay? You want to talk about anything?"

Jeremy didn't know what to say. Discord was gone, Wall-StreetBets was dark—he didn't believe in conspiracies but the timing seemed incredibly suspect. No doubt, the Discord site had been getting complaints about "hate speech," or whatever they wanted to call it, for some time. Certainly, the WSB board had dealt with ugly language since its inception. And sure, tons of people were signing up—by the millions—but Reddit was a huge site, with hundreds of millions of users. Why couldn't WSB handle a few million accounts? Was this a prelude to a bigger shutdown? Was this foreshadowing the closure of the entire WSB subreddit?

Could it really have something to do with the powerful Wall Street funds, and their efforts to shut down the short squeeze? Could it really be some sort of a first strike?

Wall Street was powerful. Firms like Melvin Capital and Citadel had billions of dollars at their disposal. Jeremy and his fellow longs were weak and small, like ants compared to Melvin. But there were millions upon millions of them, a veritable sea of ants. United, that many ants could topple just about anything.

Still, if they couldn't communicate, if they couldn't unite—

What if it really was a first strike? If you were Wall Street, and you had just fired that first strike, what would you do next? Jeremy didn't need to finish the thought, because Karl had already finished it for him, just a moment ago.

That's when you'd really hit them.

And hit them hard.

CHAPTER TWENTY-TWO

January 28, 2021

A little after 5:00 a.m.

Vlad Tenev came awake suddenly to a barrage of panicking technology; his cell phone vibrating and blinking on the table next to his bed, his laptop computer pinging frantically to itself as it was pelted by e-mail after rapid-fired e-mail; even, perhaps, a landline lost somewhere in his sprawling California home, a short commute by car or bike or skateboard from the Robinhood offices in Menlo Park.

Vlad rubbed his eyes, chasing the last vestiges of sleep away. He couldn't remember what he'd been dreaming about—no doubt something having to do with democratized finance and level playing fields, or maybe renewable energy, healthy drinking water, a living minimum wage—but it had probably involved cats, and possibly even GameStop—because by the time he'd gone to sleep the night before, everyone, everywhere, had been talking about GameStop.

He rolled over in his bed and reached for the phone first, hoping to quell the electronic onslaught before it woke his wife and toddler. He'd made it a mission in life to carve out hours in the morning for his young family, but running a quickly growing company meant he couldn't completely cut himself off from the outside world. If Robinhood's meteoric rise had taught him anything, it was that shit happened fast; close your eyes, and you never knew how much was going to change before you opened them again.

Even so, the messages—from Orlando, of all places—that Vlad saw flashing across his phone's screen caught him by surprise. Before he even realized it, he was up out of the bed and sprinting across the carpet toward his computer.

From the messages and the e-mails, it was a quick jump to a Google Hangout, where a group of his highest-level employees were already waiting for him. Jim in Orlando, of course, and a handful of execs from clearing, trading, and legal. Jim was leading the show, not only because he had the expertise to understand what the hell was going on, but because he'd already been mentally dealing with the disaster for a few hours now.

Jim had gotten the first call from his head of treasury at 5:50 a.m. East Coast time, more than three hours ago—which, in itself, had been strange. Usually, Jim was briefed every morning at 5:30 a.m. on the capital requirements that arrived, each day, at exactly 5:11 a.m. Eastern from the NSCC, a division of the DTCC, the federally regulated body tasked with overseeing Robinhood's trading and the two-day clearing process that took place between every retail trade. When the call had come in twenty minutes late, Jim had wondered if something had gone wrong; but he couldn't have predicted that it was something so unimaginable that his own team had spent the extra time trying to figure out if it was real, or some software-driven mistake.

Even after they'd spent the twenty minutes calling around

to make sure the number that had been sent over by the clearing agency was correct, Jim had made them go back and check again. Then he had called himself, speaking to his liaison at the NSCC—and only once he'd confirmed, and reconfirmed, the number had he reached out to Menlo Park.

Vlad stared at the number that now dominated a section of his computer screen, then shook his head.

$3.7 billion.

"This can't be real," someone on the hangout said, putting words to what they were all still thinking.

But the number had been checked and checked again. Overnight, the NSCC had requested—nay, demanded—*three billion, seven hundred million dollars* to cover their capital requirements for the current trading going through Robinhood's brokerage account.

Vlad tried to calm himself as he contemplated what the number meant, and how, in God's name, the NSCC could have possibly come up with such a figure. By now, though it had been a steep learning curve, he was fairly well versed on the basics of how clearing worked: When a customer bought shares in a stock on Robinhood—say, GameStop—at a specific price, the order was first sent to Robinhood's in-house clearing brokerage, who in turn bundled the trade to a market maker for execution. The trade was then brought to a clearinghouse, who oversaw the trade all the way to the settlement.

During this time period, the trade itself needed to be "insured" against anything that might go wrong, such as some sort of systemic collapse or a default by either party—although in reality, in regulated markets, this seemed extremely unlikely. While the customer's money was temporarily put aside, essentially in an untouchable safe, for the two days it took for the clearing agency to verify that both parties were able to provide what they had agreed upon—the brokerage house, Robinhood—had to insure the deal with a deposit; money of its own, separate from the money that the customer had provided, that could be used to guarantee the value of the trade. In financial parlance, this "collateral" was known as VAR—or value at risk.

For a single trade of a simple asset, it would have been relatively easy to know how much the brokerage would need to deposit to insure the situation; the risk of something going wrong would be small, and the total value would be simple to calculate. If GME was trading at $400 a share and a customer wanted ten shares, there was $4000 at risk, plus or minus some nominal amount due to minute vagaries in market fluctuations during the two-day period before settlement. In such a simple situation, Robinhood might be asked to put up $4000 and change—in addition to the $4000 of the customer's buy order, which remained locked in that safe.

The deposit requirement calculation grew more complicated as layers were added onto the trading situation. A single trade had low inherent risk; multiplied to millions of trades, the risk profile began to change. The more volatile the stock—in price and/or volume—the riskier a buy or sell became.

Of course, the NSCC did not make these calculations by hand; they used sophisticated algorithms to digest the numerous inputs coming in from the trade—type of equity, volume, current volatility, where it fit into a brokerage's portfolio as a whole—and spit out a "recommendation" of what sort of deposit would protect the trade. And this process was entirely automated; the brokerage house would continually run its trading activity through the federal clearing system and would receive its updated deposit requirements as often as every fifteen minutes while the market was open. Premarket during a trading week, that number would come in at 5:11 a.m. East Coast time, usually right as Jim, in Orlando, was finishing his morning coffee. Robinhood would then have until 10:00 a.m. to satisfy the deposit requirement for the upcoming day of trading—or risk being in default, which could lead to an immediate shutdown of all operations.

Usually, the deposit requirement was tied closely to the actual dollars being "spent" on the trades; a near equal number of buys and sells in a brokerage house's trading profile lowered its overall risk, and though volatility was common, especially in the past half-decade, even a two-day settlement period came with an acceptable level of confidence that nobody would fail to deliver on their trades.

To that respect, over the past week—even with the incredible volume of trading taking place in what were being called "meme" stocks, particularly GME—Robinhood's deposit requirements had been high, but understandable. On January 25, the deposit requirement at the start of the day had been $125 million. By the twenty-sixth, as GameStop's volume had exploded and the price had shot toward the moon, Robinhood's deposit requirement had risen to a heavy $291 million—a significant figure, beyond anything they'd seen before, but still manageable. Even after Elon Musk's tweet, and the wild volumes and price actions that had instantly occurred, Robinhood's deposit requirement with the NSCC had dropped to $282 million.

The number Vlad was looking at right now was a magnitude higher than the deposit requirement just twenty-four hours ago: *$3.7 billion.* It seemed — obscene.

When the number had first come in — and once Jim had pulled his jaw back off the floor — he'd dug into how the NSCC had come up with such a staggering figure. Once he'd gotten his liaison at the agency on the phone, he'd broken down the charge into two parts. The NSCC's algorithm had taken in all the risk inputs from the trading volumes and volatility of the day before and come up with a VAR of $1.3 billion, and had added to that an "excess capital premium charge" of an additional $2.2 billion and change. This additional charge had been added because the original VAR charge far exceeded Robinhood's net capital — thus the original call being so large that Robinhood didn't have the cash on hand to cover it had led to a multiplying effect — an additional charge to cover the risk of Robinhood not being able to cover. At the moment, Robinhood had close to $700 million on deposit with the NSCC — which left them approximately $3 billion short.

Logically, Vlad could see how the NSCC's computers might have come up with such a huge deposit requirement; not only were the retail trades coming in at a volume volatility that was unprecedented, but they were almost all on the *buy* side. There was no way to offset some of the risk with sell trades; and since GameStop was itself an inherently risky equity, with such a huge short float, the overall risk grew exponentially.

But still, Vlad had never seen or imagined anything like

this. To compare, the biggest special charge Robinhood had ever gotten from the NSCC before had been for $25 million. Now the NSCC was asking for an additional $2.2 *billion*, on top of its $1.3 billion VAR.

Once Jim had confirmed that the numbers weren't a mistake, that the charges were real and they only had until 10:00 a.m. to make good on that ungodly deposit, the question quickly became—what could they do?

First and foremost, despite what anybody might think or say or publish after the fact or scream on Twitter or Reddit or Clubhouse, Vlad believed that his main responsibility was to the Robinhood users. In line with this thinking, Vlad felt that the only option that was truly off the table was failing to meet those deposit requirements—because that would lead to a potential shutdown—meaning those users wouldn't be able to buy or sell *anything*, let alone GameStop.

Barring failure, the next option down the line was to somehow lower that deposit—to at least a dollar range that would be feasible to cover with Robinhood's existing cash and its lines of credit. To this end, Robinhood had less than five hours; and there was simply no way they could raise $3 billion in that amount of time.

But that didn't mean the situation was hopeless.

Vlad had spent the past few days watching the GameStop drama like everyone else; and despite, again, what everyone might say after the fact, he felt philosophically aligned with the retail traders. He hadn't built Robinhood for the hedge funds or the Wall Street suits; he had built it so that regular people could *compete* with the hedge funds and the Wall Street suits. And to that end, he'd succeeded: his reported

20 million users had an average age somewhere between twenty-eight and thirty-one, with an average account size of just $3500. This stood in stark contrast to even E-Trade, whose average account size was $100,000. Robinhood's base was made up of average Joes and Janes, sitting on their couches in their living rooms and dorm rooms, finding cash in between the cushions next to old slices of pizza and missing keys, and investing that money in the "stonks" they loved. Stonks like GameStop.

When people like Mark Cuban, the mega-billionaire and TV star, tweeted, as he had the day before—I got to say I LOVE LOVE what is going on with #wallstreetbets. All of those years of High Frequency Traders front running retail traders, now speed and density of information and retail trading is giving the little guy an edge. Even my 11 yr old traded w them and made $.—Vlad might well have cheered right along with him. Vlad didn't know, personally, the amateur trader calling himself DFV on Reddit who had made a fortune after doing his own diligent research into the company—but it was precisely the stories surrounding DFV's success that Robinhood had been built to enable.

So it was only after much internal, soul-scarring, deeply spiritual agony, and after much discussion with their representatives at the NSCC, that Vlad and his team came to the only conclusion they felt they could—they needed to lower the risk profile that had led to the obscene deposit requirement. To do so, they would restrict trading on a handful of stocks—specifically, they would temporarily no longer allow any Robinhood users to buy any more shares of GameStop or the thirteen other meme equities that were causing so much havoc.

It wasn't an easy decision, but it was perfectly legal—Robinhood had the right to restrict trading on any symbol for any reason, and other brokerages would be forced to act in similar fashion by what was going on in the market that week. And by restricting buying—and not selling—of an equity, Robinhood didn't feel they were hurting their users per se. Their traders could still *sell* their GameStop, they just couldn't buy—and after all, how could you *lose* money by not being able to buy a stock at what, in all likelihood, must be very close to its high?

Closing down the buy side of a stock seemed the perfect fix, because it would instantly lower the risk profile for the trading day, which would give the NSCC a new input to its algorithm; the fix was so simple, in fact, it *literally* was as easy as pressing a button—specifically, the one Vlad had right in front of him on the Robinhood dashboard that would shut down the buy and simultaneously send out an instant, automated e-mail informing the users. An operational system—that, well, maybe should have been *exceptionalized*—but one that could solve their problem in a matter of minutes.

And that was, in fact, what happened; once the decision to close down the buy side of GameStop was made, the NSCC returned to Robinhood with an updated deposit requirement. They'd entirely waived the excess capital premium charge of $2.2 billion, and arrived at a full, net deposit requirement of around $1.4 billion in total. Robinhood immediately added a bit over $700 million to the slightly under $700 million they already had on deposit and met all their requirements for the day.

Vlad leaned back from his computer, pondering what

they had just done, perhaps more than a little oblivious to what might come next. Of course, there would be consequences to stopping 20 million users from being able to buy GameStop at that particular moment in time. But wouldn't the consequences of Robinhood being shut down—of those same 20 million customers not being able to *sell* GameStop, if the stock had started to crater—have been infinitely worse?

Robinhood had met its deposit requirement. Though one could quibble about the language, the move it was making was more about compliance than "liquidity"; Robinhood was plenty liquid. The massive deposit requirement hadn't been related to margin or leverage or options, since Robinhood had already restricted those maneuvers as the weeks had progressed. The word "liquidity" didn't really apply; it was one of those "gotcha" terms used by reporters to aim blame. You couldn't *blame* Robinhood for the vagaries of T+2 clearing, or for a black swan event that had led to a $3.7 billion charge.

And you certainly couldn't blame Vlad himself, or derive baseless, wild conspiracy theories from what could easily be described as the result of a series of logical, if coincidental, occurrences.

Melvin's short position had exploded into a short squeeze because the retail traders on WallStreetBets had targeted GameStop, had bought and bought and bought, causing massive volume and price volatility. Robinhood, through which a large portion of those retail traders had bought their GameStop, had suddenly faced a massive deposit requirement because of that volatility—and had been forced to shut down buying of GameStop.

True, one could argue, this in turn would stop the rise in GameStop's stock, poking a pin into the short squeeze, potentially allowing the hedge funds to cover.

And also, true, Citadel—who BY COINCIDENCE handled most of Robinhood's trades and BY COINCIDENCE provided the lion's share of Robinhood's profits through its payment for order flow mechanism—now had a financial stake in Melvin Capital, most associated with those shorts—and had just helped lift—NOT BAIL—Melvin out of its precarious financial situation via a $2.75 billion infusion of cash along with Steve Cohen.

And also, also true, all of this had, by EVEN UNLIKELIER COINCIDENCE, happened right after the GameStop rallying cries on Discord and WallStreetBets had been, at least, temporarily, silenced or curtailed.

But from Vlad's perspective, all of this was purely circumstantial. His users might not be happy, but what Robinhood had done was, no matter how they might see it, no matter how many coincidences and conspiracy theories might stack up, really for their own good.

Vlad's job, going forward, wasn't to pontificate about conspiracy theories, or unlikely coincidences—it was simply to make sure such a thing never happened again.

PART THREE

I am not a cat.

—Keith Gill

What's an Exit Strategy?

—Keith Gill

CHAPTER TWENTY-THREE

January 28, 2021

Three minutes before market close.
Wilmington, Massachusetts.

Keeping Customers Informed
Through Market Volatility

Our mission at Robinhood is to democratize finance for all. We're proud to have created a platform that has helped everyday people, from all backgrounds, shape their financial futures and invest for the long term.

We continuously monitor the markets and make changes where necessary. In light of recent volatility, we are restricting transactions for certain securities to position closing only, including $AMC, $BB, $BBBY, $EXPR, $GME, $KOSS, $NAKD and $NOK. We also raised margin requirements for certain securities...

Keith Gill wasn't certain how he'd ended up on his back on the floor of his basement, staring up at the ceiling, as his thoughts swirled like a wild cyclone behind his eyes;

but it seemed the appropriate place to ride out the last few minutes of the craziest trading day he'd ever experienced— perhaps one of the craziest trading days in the history of the Street.

Keith still couldn't fully unpack what he'd witnessed. He knew he was not alone in this; he was not alone. On his desk, one of his screens was open to the WallStreetBets board, which had been made fully public again and was now mostly chronicling a volcanic eruption of anger, conspiracy theories, and despair; most of it revolved around Robinhood—and could be summed up by one of the many tweets Keith had stumbled upon while riffling through the site that morning, this one by another YouTuber, whose Twitter handle was @OMGitsBirdman:

> An app named "Robinhood" stealing
> from the poor and giving to the rich
> can't make this up

Keith had read Robinhood's blog post—and received their e-mail—at the same time as everyone else who had a Robinhood account; even though it was probably the result of an automated function that involved a massive mailing list, it had seemed directed squarely at him.

> We are restricting transactions for certain securities...

In Keith's mind, they should have just come right out and said it. The millions of Robinhood customers could no longer buy GameStop through the app, along with a half-dozen other meme stocks—basically anything that Melvin

Capital and their Wall Street colleagues had shorted and were trying to cover.

And it wasn't just Robinhood that had restricted buying into GME; many of the other online brokerages, such as E-Trade, Interactive Brokers, Webull, TD Ameritrade, and Schwab, had enacted varying degrees of restrictions of their own—but the one uniting feature was that all of the restrictions squarely targeted the same group of traders: regular people, on their couches and in their basements. The very people who were buying GameStop—could no longer buy GameStop.

As a brokerage firm, we have many financial requirements, including SEC net capital obligations and clearinghouse deposits. Some of these requirements fluctuate based on volatility in the markets and can be substantial in the current environment. These requirements exist to protect investors and the markets...

To the Reddit board, and across Twitter, Robinhood's announcement—via blog and e-mail—seemed immediately suspect; as much as they were trying to couch it as if it were some clinical, unemotional, perfectly acceptable maneuver, it appeared, from the outside, like a direct attempt to stifle the short squeeze in progress. Only the retail traders had been shut off, and only the buy side of GME had been shut down; institutions were free to continue to cover, which they could now do in a controlled fashion. Without the pressure of millions of Redditors buying, even as the shorts continued to cover, the stock had nowhere to go but down.

Keith had watched it all happen in real time. Premarket, the stock had momentarily crossed $500 a share—halfway to the insane $1000 price target that had been predicted all over the WSB board—and seemed utterly unstoppable. Then Robinhood had pulled the plug—and it was like a shotgun blast to the short squeeze. The stock had plunged, more than 40 percent, opening at $265 a share. From there, it had been a roller coaster—the stock descending as low as $112.25, then struggling back up toward its close, minutes away, of $193.60. If there was any question as to whether you could point squarely at Robinhood and the other on-line brokerages as to why the short squeeze had apparently imploded, you needed only to look at the daily trading volumes. With the buy side effectively squelched, the volume of shares traded had dropped to almost half of what it had been the day before; compared to Monday and Tuesday of that week, the volume had descended by two-thirds.

Robinhood and the other brokerages had already begun to indicate that they'd soon take their feet off the brakes; Robinhood would shortly allow some level of buying to begin again, now that their "capital requirements" had been met. But still, restrictions would stay in place. Robinhood's users would be able to purchase only a highly limited number of shares in GameStop—as little as a single share, for a time—which really did make it seem like the company was doing its best to end the rally for good.

Keith had watched it all happen from his basement lair with a strange sense of detachment. He still had trouble thinking of all this as something he had been involved in— let alone been responsible for. He liked to think of himself as an innocent bystander; he wasn't the first or the only person to buy GameStop, but some might say what he had started had snowballed into a movement. All he had done, in his mind, was to try to educate people through his YouTube streams and WSB posts. He had been honest throughout, hadn't advised anyone to do anything, had always made it clear that people needed to do their own research and that the market was inherently risky.

And boy, had that been an epic understatement; he was about to post his YOLO update, and even with his eyes closed, he could see the red glow of his single day's losses. At yesterday's close, his account was worth over $44 million; it had risen more than $20 million that day alone. Premarket today, it had hit a high of well over $50 million—and then, when Robinhood had pulled the plug, Keith had lost nearly half that in a matter of minutes. Even now, he'd hardly recovered; his update would show a trading account value of a little over $33 million, a loss of almost $15 million on the day.

Fifteen million gone, like smoke dissipating in a stiff wind. And yet he was still sitting on a massive fortune, the kind of money that wasn't just life changing, but potentially generational. His kids' kids would have a cushion in life if he managed it properly. He'd be able to consummate a dream he'd had since childhood—of building an indoor track in his hometown of Brockton.

He knew that many people on the WSB board were being hurt way worse than he was. Most hadn't bought GameStop anywhere near $5 a share; the vast majority had bought once the short squeeze had begun, and many had bought near the top. They were losing money—and it seemed extremely unfair.

Even the WallStreetBets board itself had taken to Twitter

to voice their dismay at the turn of events. A tweet from the moderators had been posted that morning:

Individual investors are being stripped of their ability to trade on @RobinhoodApp

Meanwhile hedge funds and institutional investors can continue to trade as normal.

What do you call a market that removes retail investors ability to buy to save institutional investors shorts?

And it was clear that the anger was no longer confined to the WSB community but had blown out into the real world and was spreading rapidly through the mainstream. Voices across all forms of social media were decrying what appeared to be 2008 all over again—Wall Street being bailed out, while big institutions used their power to stomp on the little guy. But because of social media, the little guy now had a voice, and many, many champions—not just YouTube celebrities or esoteric billionaires, but even high-level members of government.

Responding to a tweet by *Motherboard*, Vice's tech newsletter, about the situation, Democratic House Representative Alexandria Ocasio-Cortez had responded in a tweet of her own:

This is unacceptable. We now need to know more about @Robinhoodapp's decision to block retail investors from purchasing stock while hedge funds are freely able to trade the stock as they see fit. As a member of the Financial Services CMTe, I'd support a hearing if necessary.

Her tweet had led to a rare agreement from Senator Ted Cruz: Fully Agree.

Over on CNBC, Elizabeth Warren, the former presidential candidate and Massachusetts senator, had trashed the SEC for not stepping in: "We need an SEC that has clear rules about market manipulation and then has the backbone to get in and enforce those rules."

And Representative Maxine Waters, chairman of the House Committee on Financial Services, had gone a step further, already calling for a hearing on the situation. *A congressional hearing!* What did that even mean? Keith had read about congressional hearings in the newspaper, had seen snippets of them on the news and on the Web. Important people sitting at long desks surrounded by lawyers, taking turns answering questions hurled at them by the most powerful people in the country. How could they possibly build a hearing about what was happening right that moment? Who could they possibly call to testify? Robinhood, sure, maybe Melvin? Who else? Some college kid calling himself buttplug59 on a subreddit? Mark Cuban's eleven-year-old son? A dude with a mullet and a bandanna and a YouTube livestream?

It was hard to imagine what such a hearing might accomplish. If the goal would be to try to encapsulate the unfairness of what appeared to be happening, and the fury such a moment had inspired, it might have been simpler just to spend a few moments following David Portnoy, the Barstool Sports mogul's Twitter feed. He seemed to have continued his role of taking on the mantle of speaking for the WSB Reddit crowd, in a barrage of new, unhinged video posts he'd made that afternoon. Dressed in a white

T-shirt and raving at the camera like he'd just escaped from a mental hospital, he'd made it clear from the start—as a GME shareholder—where he stood:

"Everybody on Wall Street who had a hand in today's crime needs to go to prison."

From there, it had only gotten worse:

"The way they have cheated, stolen, robbed everyday people who have invested with Robinhood and other etrade accounts...by saying hey hedge funds are getting smoked, billionaires are getting smoked, so we are no longer going to let you trade certain stocks. We are shutting it off. You can't buy those stocks anymore, you can only sell them. We are going to crash those stocks so all our hedge fund billionaire friends can get out and not get killed...One of the most remarkable, illegal, shocking robberies in the history, in plain sight...just right in your face, put a gun in your mouth...Robinhood, crooks, JAIL! Ken Griffin, Citadel, JAIL! Steve Cohen, the Mets owner, JAIL!

"They are robbing you! They are stealing from you! This is criminal."

Portnoy's rant had actually gone meta, later in the day, when Steve Cohen had objected to being included in Portnoy's lineup of bad actors. On Twitter, Cohen had responded, a little before two in the afternoon:

Hey Dave, what's your beef with me. I'm just trying to make a living just like you. Happy to take this offline.

But Portnoy hadn't nearly been ready to back down. His response was fired off so fast, it was riddled with typos:

I don't do offline. That's where shady shit happens. You bailed out Melviin cause he's you're boy along with Citadel. I think you had strong hand in todays criminal events to save hedge funds at the cost of ordinary people. Do you unequivocally deny that?

Cohen's response had been filled with appropriate, and carefully worded, dismay:

What are you talking about? I unequivocally deny that accusation. I had zero to do with what happened today. BTW, if I want to make an additional investment with somebody that is my right if it's in the best interest of my investors. Chill out.

By 3:13 in the afternoon, Portnoy had calmed down, but he wasn't letting Cohen or any of the rest off the hook:

By the way I don't belive @stevenacohen2 at all. But I have no way to prove anything. But in my experience where there is smoke there is usually fire.

Keith understood—Portnoy was voicing what everyone on WSB was thinking. Portnoy was sitting on a much larger investment in GME than most of them, but his sentiments could have come from any one of the millions of board members who were watching the stock price tumble: "I'll lose 2 millin in this thing. I'm not selling. I'll eat the 2 million. I'll eat it like cake. Not selling because selling is what those fuckign assholes want me to do. I'm not going to do it. I'd rather go bankrupt…"

It was the mantra of diamond hands—but Keith understood better than anyone, "hodling" became much more difficult when the other side seemed to be capable of changing the rules with the touch of a button. Keith wouldn't have gone as far as Portnoy—he wasn't accusing Cohen, or even Citadel, of having anything to do with Robinhood's actions. But that didn't mean Portnoy was alone in voicing the opinion that something sketchy was going on. The uproar—and conspiracy theories—had gotten so loud that Citadel itself responded, to CNBC, in true legalize:

"Citadel Securities has not instructed or otherwise caused any brokerage firm to stop, suspend, or limit trading or otherwise refuse to do business. Citadel Securities remains focused on continuously providing liquidity to our clients across all market conditions."

But that wasn't going to reassure anyone watching the market chaos, and wondering why the hell they couldn't buy GME, while hedge funds like Melvin were still perfectly able to. Robinhood couldn't have made the decision lightly—despite how clinical they'd made it sound in their e-mail and blog post. They'd done incalculable damage to their reputation; already, thousands of people were slamming the company on the various app stores—Apple, Google, etc.—giving it one-star review after one-star review. Many more were threatening to leave the app and take their trading money elsewhere.

And the pushback wasn't contained to reviews, comments, and tweets by Robinhood's users; according to CNET, a lawsuit had already been filed in the Southern District of New York, and more suits were being threatened and planned. Many wanted Robinhood to pay a hefty price for limiting trading on GameStop, which begged the question even more—were they really simply responding to a deposit requirement call from the national clearing facility? Or was something nefarious truly going on?

For Keith, lying on the floor of his basement, these were heady thoughts. He'd fallen for a stock—and now billionaires and Internet moguls and US congresswomen and senators were shouting at each other all over the Internet. He wanted to stay above the fray, keep his thoughts pure and his focus on the deep, deep value—but the question Portnoy and others were asking was hard to ignore: *Why did coincidences always seem to benefit the people in power?*

At the same time, Keith was determined to stay the course. He'd liked GameStop at $5 a share when nobody else was listening to him, and he still liked it at close to $200.

Robinhood couldn't restrict the buy side forever. Citadel and Melvin and Cohen had money and power, expensive suits and Wall Street offices; Keith had a poster of a cat on his wall and a bandanna around his head.

And despite that YOLO update he was about to release, with all those zeros lined up and the commas between—Keith had started with nothing. And when you start with nothing, you have nothing to lose.

CHAPTER TWENTY-FOUR

January 29, 2021

A day later, seven hundred miles south.

The dull pounding at the door had been going on for a good five minutes before Jeremy lifted his head from his desk, where he'd set it down sometime between market close and the *Makise Kurisu Ending* of *Steins;Gate*, his favorite entry in the *Science Adventure* visual interactive novel series, which he'd played so many times that even though the dialogue was entirely in Japanese, he was pretty sure he understood much, if not all, of what was happening. Even so, the vibrant manga and subtle twists in the narrative—which leaned heavily into themes like the relative nature of time, the dissociation that came with moments of trauma, and the dangerous effect even the smallest, seemingly inconsequential action can have on the future—were no match for the waves of stress-induced mental exhaustion that had finally overtaken him as he'd watched the last wild minutes of the wildest market day of the wildest week in recent Wall Street memory finally tick away.

Head still inches from his desk, eyes shut, the image behind his eyelids was from his trading account, not the manga game, which was running in its own window on his laptop. GME had just closed at $325 a share, down from a daily high of $413.98, but still far above the dip that had occurred after Robinhood had first closed buying of the stock the day before. Even though now most restrictions had been lifted—according to the business press, Robinhood was in the process of raising a mind-numbing $3.4 billion in three days to cover any future deposit issues—the stock hadn't quite threatened the $500 ceiling again. Still, Jeremy's account showed a majestic six-figure profit.

He should have been jumping up and down, doing calisthenics, dancing to Japanese pop; but instead, he was barely able to finally open his eyes, and stare angrily toward the door of his apartment as the pounding grew and grew.

"Go away," he shouted, but that only seemed to make the person on the other side more determined. Which was as much evidence as Jeremy needed for him to guess who was interrupting his self-imposed seclusion.

Which also meant he had little choice. The door, or Jeremy—Casper wasn't going away until one of them broke down and let him in.

Jeremy sighed, then rose from his desk and navigated past the piles of laundry, delivery cartons and bags from a half-dozen ordered-in meals, and a metropolis of discarded plastic Gatorade, water, and soda bottles that covered every open surface between him and his front entrance.

He'd only gotten the door halfway open before Casper was inside, pushing past him, two heavy grocery bags in his arms. He set the bags on the couch, between two empty pizza boxes, then looked around at the mess.

"I really like what you've done with the place. Can't wait to see you on the cover of *Shut-In Weekly*."

Jeremy closed the door, wishing his brother were still on the other side.

"What do you want, Casper?"

"Wellness check, buddy."

"Dad sent you?"

Casper shook his head. He came around the couch, pushed one of the grocery bags aside just enough to give him room to sit down.

"Nope. Karl texted me, said you missed last night's study session. And Michael says you weren't in class today or yesterday."

Jeremy rubbed his eyes. He'd been ignoring his friends' texts and e-mails, so he should have figured one of them might reach out to Casper. For all Jeremy knew, they'd been down to his apartment to see what was going on with him; he'd had the music up loud for much of the day.

"And I noticed the car hasn't been moved since last week. Which means you also missed your Covid test."

Jeremy cursed. He'd completely forgotten about that. He and Casper shared the one car, which was parked in a garage two blocks from Jeremy's apartment. The spots weren't assigned, and the garage was usually busy—which meant the car never ended up parked in the same place. Of course, Casper would notice—the kid had a mind like a filing cabinet.

The way he was looking around Jeremy's apartment, there was no question he was calculating how long Jeremy had kept himself locked inside; how many meals he'd had delivered, how many Zoom classes he'd probably missed.

Knowing Casper, he'd already seen the stack of school text-books on Jeremy's desk, still in the same position from the week before. Unopened, because Jeremy had barely done any schoolwork at all in days.

Again and again, Jeremy had promised himself he'd stop watching GameStop, stop reading the WSB board; that he was going to hold for a year anyway, so the day-by-day fluctuations were just noise he could tune out. But whenever he'd tried to concentrate on something else—like a problem set—he'd find his eyes wandering back to his phone or his laptop, and then he'd be right back onto the board, or in his Robinhood account.

He'd been staring at the screen when Elon Musk had tweeted Gamestonk!! and had watched the after-hours price spiral toward the moon. He'd still been online thirteen hours later, when in premarket the stock had eclipsed $500 a share—and his account value had reached $175,000. And he'd been on the WallStreetBets board, reading comments, when the Robinhood blog post had gone up—and all hell had broken loose.

A day later, the stock had grudgingly recovered, but there was no doubt that the short squeeze had been interrupted. Whether it could regain its footing—whether there were enough shorts left and enough diamond hands opposing them to push the stock back into the stratosphere—was un-known. But there was no doubt—Jeremy could no longer look away. Even his beloved anime couldn't compete with the drama going on with GME.

"At least I know it's not a girl," Casper said, gingerly moving a piece of uneaten pizza from beneath him on the couch. "So what the hell is going on, man?"

Jeremy glanced past his brother toward the laptop. Casper followed his eyes. Though the anime was still the brightest thing on the screen, his open trading account and the WSB board were just as recognizable, even from across the room.

"Christ, man. You haven't sold yet? I told you to fucking sell."

"Yes, you told me to sell at twenty dollars. And then you told me to sell at thirty. And then at a hundred, like Dad."

"So what's it at now?"

Jeremy crossed back toward the desk.

"Closed around three twenty-five."

There was a pause.

"Holy shit, man."

Casper rose from the couch and followed Jeremy, who was already dropping back into his desk chair.

"I mean," Casper said, "holy shit. You're rich. Or—you would be if you sold."

"I'm not selling."

Jeremy hadn't meant it to come out so harsh. His heart was pounding faster than it needed to, and he could feel his hands balling into fists. He wasn't sure what was making him so angry. He knew his brother was just worried about him. But Casper didn't understand what was going on. He wasn't on the WSB board, day and night, reading the rallying cries, being bolstered by the camaraderie. He didn't understand that Jeremy was part of a community, more than that, part of a tribe.

Jeremy had seen some posts by people who had sold—people who'd taken profits because they were afraid, or felt betrayed by what Robinhood had done, or believed that

Wall Street was going to find a way to win, one way or another—and Jeremy had truly felt betrayed, just as he had when his dad had sold. He knew it wasn't fair—he didn't know these people, didn't know what sorts of hardships they were facing and what it meant to them to make a few hundred dollars, or a few thousand, or tens of thousands on a stock. But he had truly believed that those who were still holding were in this together.

"If we stick together as a community, keep holding," he said, his voice calmer now, "the stock will go up."

"Yeah, maybe. And maybe it won't. Maybe it will drop right back to $40, or $20, or $10. But what I do know is that if you keep this up, you're going to lose the few friends you say you have. And you're definitely going to flunk out of school."

"Brothers are awesome," Jeremy responded.

Casper smiled. Then he shook his head.

"You can pretend that you're doing this because you're a part of some movement, some community that matters to you—and maybe that's true. But I know you, Jeremy, which means I know how this is going to play out."

"What do you mean?"

"Bottle caps, man."

Jeremy glanced back at his brother, who was leaning over his shoulder now, reading the WSB board. *Bottle caps.* It was a memory from back on the boat, when they were two kids who really only had each other, because there were never any other kids around. They'd invented numerous games and competitions to keep themselves occupied.

Jeremy wasn't sure which one of them had first started collecting bottle caps; but almost immediately, it had become a sport—seeing whose collection could grow the biggest, with the best, most exotic caps. Every island they'd stopped on, the two of them would rush ahead of their parents, scouring the streets, gutters, sidewalks for those little circular flecks of metal.

Within a few weeks, both of their collections had grown impressive—filling their mother's empty shoe boxes, their dad's unused tackle boxes, even the plastic buckets they'd used to clean the canvas of the deck. And they'd been about even until they'd reached the Bahamas, making port in Nassau for a monthlong stay.

That first day on the island, Jeremy and his brother had headed out looking for more bottle caps. An hour in, walking in the hot sun, they hadn't found any for their collection. They'd been standing in the street—two kids, seven and nine years old—when Casper had noticed they were in front of a bar. The place had looked seedy, with a neon beer sign in the window. Jeremy had told him they should head back to the boat, but Casper had only given him a look, and then run inside.

Jeremy had wanted to follow but had stayed rooted where he was. Maybe he'd been scared; maybe he'd figured it was a waste of time. Casper was seven and didn't have any money. But to Jeremy's surprise, just a moment later Casper had come running back out, a giant grin on his face. In his hands—a bottle of Red Stripe. Not only did he have the winning bottle cap, but the entire beer.

"Look," Casper said. "I was wrong and you were right. You got your short squeeze. You made over a hundred thousand dollars. And now you're going to lose every penny of it. Because—and I mean this in the nicest way—you guys on this board are a bunch of losers. And the guys you're up against are sharks. They *win*—that's what they do. You're up right now, but you'll hold all the way back down."

Jeremy stared at his brother.

"You think Melvin Capital gives a crap about *community*, or some 'movement'? You think Citadel cares about whose 'turn it is'? They'd cut all your throats, dance in your blood, then walk away without a second thought. They're winners. You're a loser. And that's why I know you're going to pull a loss out of this win."

Casper gave a last look at the WSB board, then turned away and headed for the door. Jeremy watched him go, thinking about Melvin, Citadel, and bottle caps.

It wasn't until his brother was gone, and Jeremy was alone in the room, that he realized Casper was right.

* * *

Forty-eight hours later, Jeremy was back in the exact same spot, but now he was standing, his entire body trembling as he hovered over the screen of his phone, lying right next to his computer's keyboard. His hair was wild and the music was playing well past 11. Not Kanako Itō this time, but Zwei, more techno-rock than pop, Megu's dramatic bass guitar riffs melding with Ayumu's vocals, waves of sound crashing against the walls of Jeremy's apartment as he counted the minutes to market open, after the longest, most difficult weekend of his entire life.

Once his decision to sell had been made, he'd been determined to stay off the computer. Beginning right after his brother had left, and all the way past midnight Friday, he'd lain on his couch, eyes closed, willing himself to think of anything other than GameStop.

Saturday, he'd taken half a dozen walks around the grounds of his apartment complex. He'd sat by the lake, watching birds chase each other through the stone gray air. He'd even pulled up a plastic recliner by the pool and had sat there, bundled up against the midwinter chill, hoping nobody he knew would happen by, but knowing even if they had, they'd probably have avoided him anyway. And not just because of Covid; Jeremy knew full well that he looked like a madman, because he really did feel like he was on his way to going mad.

By Saturday afternoon, despite his best intentions, he'd ended up back on his computer. As he'd expected, most of what he saw on the WSB board were diamond hands pumping, propping each other up to remain strong for the coming week. A couple of the posts were truly inspiring; perhaps the most vivid of them all was a post put up by user SomeGuyInDeutschland containing a high-res video of a billboard someone had bought in Times Square, which simply read "$GME GO BRRR" over a Robinhood-like stock graph going vertical. The billboard, playing off the popular meme of the sound made when a machine prints money, quickly became the top post on the board and the No. 2 post on Reddit overall. Another post that connected to Jeremy on a more personal level was an image put up by a user calling himself or herself Parliament containing characters from *Teenage Mutant Ninja Turtles*. In one frame, one of the turtles is pictured as a young child, being led by the hand by Master Splinter, the turtles' rodent mentor. In the second frame, the same turtle is now a muscled adult, guiding along Splinter, who is now aged and humbled. Superimposed over the turtle in both frames, the word "Millennials," and over Splinter, "GameStop."

Jeremy had understood the meme immediately; it played on his sense of nostalgia, how GameStop was once the place he'd begged his parents to take him to, a place he could stay for hours, checking out the descriptions on the backs of game boxes, playing demos, reading gaming magazines. Now it was Jeremy's turn to give back to the company, show his appreciation and love.

But the meme that really spoke to Jeremy, above all the others, was a minute-long scene from the animated movie *The Iron Giant*, posted by a user named jeepers_sheepers, which had been repurposed via subtitles. In the scene, the giant robot flies into space to protect the earth—and a little kid—from a missile. Through the subtitles, the story reads a little differently: The kid is now all the normal people who own GameStop, the weak hands who are ready to sell; the Iron Giant represents the WSB diamond hands. And the missile—Melvin Capital. The giant goes up to protect the kid, blowing up the missile—and the ensuing explosion reads: "Bankruptcy."

Watching the video, over and over, Jeremy felt just like that kid—and the WSB community was protecting him as he waited through that torturous weekend for the market to reopen.

Jeremy wanted to be part of history, and he wanted to keep holding like the rest—he truly felt that he would disappoint these people he didn't know and would never meet if he sold. But his brother had been right—Jeremy wasn't a shark. He didn't even know how to win properly. Given time, he'd eventually turn this win into a loss.

And besides, he rationalized to himself, many of those diamond hands on WSB had gotten in much later than him; at $100, $200, even $300 and higher. They had different anchoring positions. His baseline was less than $17. Shoot for the moon? *He'd already hit the moon.*

And now he was going to prove his brother wrong. He was going to *win*.

He let the techno-rock fill him up from the inside as he counted the last few minutes until 9:30 a.m., and then he brought his finger down on the Sell button on his Robinhood account.

A total of 350 shares—which he'd bought at an average of a little over $17—sold, at $314.22 a share, for $109,977.

Jeremy stepped back from his desk. And then his entire body started to move, his pipe cleaner arms and legs jerking and jagging to the Japanese music, like the limbs of a marionette whose strings had gotten tangled in a ceiling fan.

He'd done it. He was out. He was dancing.

And he would continue to dance, until eventually, he would stop long enough to call his brother, to tell him the news, and then even longer, to call his father, to apologize.

And then he would dance some more.

CHAPTER TWENTY-FIVE

Three days later

There was a brief moment of weightlessness as the narrow-bodied Delta Airbus A220 bounced and bounded through the last few tendrils of the storm that had gathered, quite suddenly, over Phoenix's Sky Harbor Airport—and then Kim felt herself pressed back into her seat as the engines kicked in, the silvery capsule around her punching through the thick canopy of clouds and into a spectacularly clear, blue morning sky.

Kim was breathing hard behind her mask as she watched the clouds recede through the cold glass oval window to her left, and she could feel her heart racing in her chest. Flying had never bothered her before; she'd made this trip a dozen times in the past five years, and it was about as seamless a hop as modern air travel allowed. She'd normally leave Phoenix shortly after breakfast, be back at work at the hospital by lunch. But like everything else in this year of Covid, what used to be routine now seemed alien.

The masks, the temperature check at the gate, the fact that there was nobody sitting in the middle seat next to her—well, at least that was an improvement, though she felt certain it would be the most temporary of the new standards. Already she'd read that some airlines had begun hedging on such valuable, if medieval, on-board real estate. Kim was only surprised it had taken them so long. Not even a deadly virus could stand up very long against receding airline profits. The machine, as always, needed to be fed.

Now that they were above the clouds, Kim turned away from the window. Her tray table was still up and safely stored, her laptop on the floor beneath the seat in front of her—but her phone was in her pocket. She resisted the urge to pull it out, because the seat belt sign was still on and the plane was still rising, which meant the wireless probably wasn't working yet. And besides, the market had been open only a few minutes.

Still, it was painful to be stuck in one of the few remaining disconnected spots on the planet, especially considering all that had happened in the past few days. Turbulence didn't even begin to describe what she had been through since Robinhood had turned off the spigot and dampened the short squeeze. For all she knew, by the time her flight home from Phoenix reached cruising altitude, her moonshot rocket ship was going to be more like Skylab, ending up little more than a crater in the desert 30,000 feet below where she was sitting.

By coincidence, she'd been on a similar plane going in the opposite direction on January 28, when Robinhood had put the brakes on GameStop, which had been hovering close to its $500 a share high. That morning, she'd almost canceled her trip, even though she'd been looking forward to the week in Phoenix visiting her best friend, Angie, for nearly a year.

The days leading up to Robinhood's devastating move had been like an incredible dream. She'd watched her account rise from its initial $5000 value to $50,000, all from those 100 shares of GameStop that she'd bought for around $1600.

When the stock had touched $500 in premarket that Thursday, seven days ago, it had seemed like nothing was going to stop the rise. The short squeeze she'd explained to Chinwe was really, finally in full swing—and a price of $1000 no longer seemed like a fantasy. Paying for Brian's braces had morphed, in her mind, into the possibility that she might pay off her house. Maybe even buy a new car. Hell, anything seemed possible.

And at work, most of her colleagues had celebrated with her. A few of the girls had even followed her into the trade, buying at $200 and $300 a share; one of the night shift nurses, who had learned of Kim's good fortune, had even grabbed two shares that Wednesday night, at over $340. For people who made the kind of money they did, it was a risky move—but then again, how often did an RN at a psychiatric hospital get a chance to make life-changing profits?

Among her friends, only Chinwe had remained skeptical, or as he put it—realistic.

"Goliath just getting started," he'd say whenever he saw her in the break room.

Each time, Kim had told him to lighten up; but eventually he had broken her down just enough that late Wednesday night, she had put in a sell order for just 5 of her shares—and even after Robinhood's terrible maneuver, she'd managed to pull out a little more than her initial investment, leaving the remaining 95 shares to ride through the roller coaster that came next.

When she'd headed to the airport on the twenty-eighth, she'd honestly believed that by the time she'd landed in Phoenix, she'd be a wealthy woman.

The plane banked to the left and then finally straightened out. The seat belt light went off with a ding, followed by the soft tones of the pilot, reassuring them that they were on their way to a smooth, short flight back to California. It was another oddity, how quiet the cabin seemed. Perhaps it had to do with the masks, or perhaps the shared anxiety. Everyone had always been nervous on planes, but now people seemed more afraid of the invisible germs flying along in the canned air next to them than the possibility of a plummet followed by a crash.

Kim wasn't afraid of either. She'd been vaccinated against the first, and she'd already experienced the second—because despite what she'd thought when she'd first read the Robinhood blog and seen the reaction on the WSB board, the GME ride had never been the same again.

When Kim had first learned that Robinhood had restricted buying, the consequences hadn't quite hit her. Sure, the downward pressure took some of the steam off the short squeeze, but she'd always assumed it would be temporary, and she knew from reading WallStreetBets that the community was determined to see it through. Anyone who talked about selling was roundly ridiculed, and the peer pressure, along with the recognition that this was now a national story, driving millions and millions of new members to WallStreetBets and to GameStop, should have kept the rocket heading skyward.

And for a time, Kim had remained cautiously optimistic. Friday the twenty-ninth, the stock had remained strong, closing at $325. Then the following Monday, February 1, it had still opened strong—a hair above $316. And that's when things had started to deflate.

By the end of day, the stock had fallen to $225. And over the next two days—freefall. That morning, when she'd left Phoenix, it had been sitting at a little above $91. Still well higher than when she'd bought at $16, but less than 20 percent of the high near $500 that the stock had been trading at before Robinhood had pulled the plug.

Somewhere between $300 and $100 was when Kim had really started to get angry. Chinwe had always liked to say that there wasn't a conspiracy theory that Kim didn't love, but at first, her mind hadn't gone that way at all. She just couldn't believe that anyone could act as brazenly as Robinhood had—right in the open, for everyone to see— if something nefarious had been behind their move. But the more her anger multiplied, and the more she read Wall-StreetBets, the more she'd become convinced—when you added Robinhood's restrictions to the actions of Discord and the temporary blockage of the WSB board, it really did feel like a coordinated attack.

Whatever it was, it had certainly ruined Kim's vacation week. From the moment Angie had picked her up at the airport, Kim had been ranting about GameStop—and she hadn't let up for seven full days. The fact that she'd come to Phoenix for an inaugural party for the charitable group she and Angie had worked so hard to join—the Daughters of the American Revolution—had only made matters worse. When GME was riding high, Kim had fantasized about the checks she would be able to write toward patriotic causes like supporting female veterans, or educational sessions promoting the US Constitution. But in light of what she'd just witnessed—which more and more, she was beginning to believe was yet another blow against fairness and a level playing field—things she most equated with American patriotism—it all felt somehow sullied.

By the end of the week, even Angie, her biggest supporter, who had been so proud that Kim was part of what was going on with GameStop, had been telling her she needed to take what profits she'd made and get out. And yet somehow, Kim just couldn't sell. Even as the stock continued to fall, that very morning—she still couldn't force herself to dump her GME.

After Angie had dropped her off at the airport and she'd worked her way through the security theater—and the additional Covid double encore—she'd paused at the gate to call Chinwe, her work husband, because like a real husband and wife, they always liked to call each other before and after flights.

To her surprise, he hadn't immediately jumped on her with comments about Goliath or David; but the quiet on the other end of the line made her feel even more foolish somehow. Of all people, she thought, standing there in the Phoenix Airport, her DAR pin still stuck proudly to a corner of her lapel, she should have known better.

"I'm an idiot," she'd said into the phone. "It's okay, Chinwe. You can say it."

He'd paused on the other end.

"I don't think you're an idiot. I think you wanted to believe. And I'm proud of you for that."

His words had hit her harder than she'd expected. They were talking about GameStop. A stupid video game company.

"So should I sell?" she'd asked after a moment.

And then he'd laughed.

"I can't tell you what to do. Nobody tells you what to do."

Now, sitting in the cabin of that plane, 30,000 feet above the desert, waiting for her wireless to connect, she thought about his words. Chinwe was right—nobody had ever been able to tell her what to do. That was probably why her life was so messy. People, institutions, society—things just kept letting her down—but even so, she kept believing, and she kept charging forward.

Her world might always be unfair, and her life might always be messy. But a big part of her *liked* messy.

And the truth was, when that wireless finally powered up, Kim wasn't sure if she was going to sell, hold—or hell, maybe even buy more.

CHAPTER TWENTY-SIX

February 15, 2021

One week later.

Two a.m.

The snow was coming down in sheets as Sara stood at the end of the gravel driveway in front of her rented condo, pulling her husband's ski jacket tight over her shoulders and as far around her growing belly as she could manage. None of her own jackets fit anymore, and though she'd been browsing Amazon for weeks for pregnancy clothes, she had rarely been willing to pull the trigger. Spending money on something so temporary seemed somehow wrong; but when she thought about it, wasn't everything about this moment they were living—quite apart from the pregnancy—temporary? And where, exactly, did the definition of temporary start to fray? Nine months? A year?

She shivered, jamming her hands deep into her husband's coat pockets. The fingers of her right hand touched her phone, but she didn't draw it out into the cold. For the first time in days, she no longer felt the pull to look at its screen. Not only because it was so late on a Saturday night, or so early on a Sunday morning—which meant the market was closed, and even the WallStreetBets board, with its many millions of new users, was quiet. But because Sara knew that, for her, much of the spell had been broken.

Unlike many on the WSB board, she'd never truly given in to the delusions, the fantasies, or the daydreams; she'd always approached her trade, as small as it was in the grand scheme of things, as something grounded. But she had allowed herself to hope, and it had been hard not to get caught up in the thrill of the moment, watching the stock fire upward, toward the moon. But when reality had come crashing down—and the powers that be had once again *been*—Sara had quickly fallen back to the emotions that had become so familiar over the past year. Disappointment, acceptance, perseverance. She hadn't sold her shares, and she doubted now that she ever would.

She looked down at her feet, toward the gravel that she knew was there but could no longer see. It had been snowing for only a few hours, but already the flakes had gotten heavy and thick, accumulating in clumps and drifts that looked like dunes in the soft light from the front steps of her home, which she'd left on when she'd come outside. It hadn't been difficult, crawling out of bed at that hour without waking her husband. It was something she'd gotten good at over the course of her pregnancy. She supposed the insomnia was just another evolutionary gift, her body preparing her for the sleeplessness she'd endure after the baby was born. But tonight, she didn't really mind.

The insomnia, the sleeplessness involved with bringing something new into the world—it was just another example of reality encroaching into what could sometimes seem like a fantasy. Like a snowstorm hitting on Valentine's Day, ruining the plans they'd set to take a drive to Emmon's Lake and picnic in their car.

But the evening hadn't been a bust at all; instead of a picnic, her husband had cooked dinner, and they'd even opened a bottle of wine, which he'd had to tend to himself, because of her condition. It had been romantic and lovely and fun. Even now, standing out in the driveway, watching the snow fall, she could think of it and smile.

Her fingers still rested against her phone, but even that didn't affect the feeling of warmth spreading through her, despite the snow touching down in her hair, on her cheeks, against the bare skin at the back of her neck.

Her ten shares of GameStop were sitting at one-sixth the price she'd bought them at; but they were still hers. And if the wild, improbable, impossible ride was really over, if the moment really had been temporary, like the snowstorm swirling around her, or the current state of her body, or the moment they were all living through? Would that really change anything?

She shook her head, then started back up her snowbound driveway, toward her front steps.

Even for a realist like her, it was hard to think clearly in the middle of a snowy night. She knew things would look different, once the storm had passed, and she was finally able to see things in the bright light of day.

CHAPTER TWENTY-SEVEN

February 18, 2021

Noon.

Gabe Plotkin stared into the icy glow of his computer's digital eye, waiting for the smoke to clear, imagining the faces queuing up, one after another, in offices, homes, second homes, in cities and states spread from one coast to the other. A vast, interconnected spiderweb of powerful people, brought together for a livestream that had been described, in the press, as mostly investigative—but from Gabe's perspective, it must have seemed more a Shakespearean Greek chorus, formed for the direct purpose of sitting in judgment.

Ironic—that the worst moment of Gabe's career, and most likely one of the most painful episodes in his life, would culminate in a livestream to be aired on the Web, captured in ink for all time, available to anyone with an Internet connection. Over his career, Gabe had taken great pains to avoid any real public imprint; unlike some of his peers, even his former boss, he had never chased notoriety or willingly made public waves. Until a few months ago, hardly anyone outside his industry even knew his name.

And now here he was, making his debut in front of a world stage, expected to explain one of the biggest and quickest losses in financial history to a hungry and homebound audience. Try as he might assuage himself with his sports-based mantra—that getting back up after a fall proved character and separated the great from the merely lucky—it was hard to see past the depths of that plummet; now, dragged out in the open by a congressional committee, he had to try and explain how it had all happened, when he himself was still attempting to digest what had gone so horribly wrong.

His body stiffened as he watched that screen. It wasn't really smoke, of course; more of a pearl gray blur of pixels, and when it finally did resolve, in the center sat Maxine Waters, the chair of the House Committee on Financial Services. She was in front of a stark white background, empty save for an American flag and a framed picture hidden by her own countenance. The congresswoman looked as serious as ever as she started with the title of the day's hearing:

"Game Stopped? Who Wins and Loses When Short Sellers, Social Media, and Retail Investors Collide."

From there, she dove headfirst into it:

"Recent market volatility has put a national spotlight on institutional practices by Wall Street firms, and prompted discussion about the evolving role of technology and social media in our markets. These events have illuminated potential conflicts of interest and the predatory ways that certain funds operate, and they have demonstrated the enormous power of social media in our markets. They have also raised issues involving gamification of trading, potential harm to retail investors..."

Many of her words landed like blows on Gabe's shoulders, even though some might think them unfair. There had been nothing predatory about Melvin's short position in GameStop. It had been a simple, uncontroversial trade. In a million years, he could not have guessed that shorting a brick-and-mortar, mall-based dinosaur with massive debt and seemingly no real plan for the future would be something he would have to defend.

"Many Americans feel that the system is stacked against them," Waters continued, "and no matter what, Wall Street always wins. In this instance, many retail investors appeared motivated by a desire to beat Wall Street at its own game. And, given the losses that many retail investors have sustained as a result of volatility in the system, there are many whose belief that the system is rigged against them has been reinforced…"

If Gabe hadn't been trapped in his chair—nothing visible to the camera save a drawn window shade behind him, along with a shadowy wall and a Hewlett-Packard printer, as if he were broadcasting from a seldom-used supply closet at Melvin Capital—moments away from being called to testify, he might have turned off the livestream right there. *Losses sustained by retail investors as a result of volatility?* If the WallStreetBets mob had suffered losses, whose fault was that? Who had caused the volatility in the system?

And if the system really was rigged against the Reddit crowd, then why had Gabe just lost a reported $6 billion in a matter of days?

But Gabe had no choice except to listen, in silence, until it was his turn to unmute his camera. As he was finally called upon to speak, there was a brief pause, his eyes widening.

Perhaps nausea flowed through him as he faced this odd moment of reckoning in front of, arguably, the most powerful committee in Congress—not to mention the millions of people watching, in the only instance in history when viewing a congressional livestream was a pretty reasonable way for anyone to spend a Thursday afternoon.

"I want to make clear at the outset," he started, after thanking the committee for dragging him out into the open like this; then he went right to the heart of the matter—Robinhood's restriction of the buy side of GME, "that Melvin Capital played absolutely no role in those trading platforms' decisions. In fact, Melvin closed out all of its positions in GameStop days before those platforms put those limitations in place. Like you, we learned about those limits from news reports..."

There was no need to connect the obvious dots—that if Melvin had been out of its short position, they'd had nothing to gain from Robinhood limiting the buying of GameStop. Had Gabe known Robinhood and the other brokerages would make such a maneuver, wouldn't he have waited another day, and saved himself billions of dollars? *Who, really, was the victim here anyway?*

"Contrary to many reports," he continued, "Melvin Capital was not 'bailed out'...Citadel proactively reached out to become a new investor..."

Was it Gabe's fault that Citadel suddenly saw a hedge fund that had lost half of its value as a good investment?

"It was an opportunity for Citadel to 'buy low,'" Gabe rationalized, adding, "To be sure, Melvin was managing through a difficult time...we were not seeking a cash infusion..."

It was like defending himself with a shotgun, attempting to blast holes in the conspiratorial narrative that had been building on social media for the past two weeks. And while he was defending Melvin, he found himself also needing to use that shotgun to defend one of Wall Street's most controversial tools.

"When our research suggests a company will not live up to expectations and its stock price is overvalued, we might 'short' a stock...when the markets go down, we have a duty to protect our investors' capital."

With GME, the ground beneath that trade couldn't have been firmer.

"Specific to GameStop, we had a research-supported view well before the recent events. In fact, we had been short GameStop since Melvin's inception six years earlier because we believed and still believe that its business model..."

But Gabe had to know that for much of his audience, the rationale fell on deaf ears. They weren't looking for financial education; they were looking for someone to blame. Although only a handful of the congressional inquisitors took direct aim at him during the proceedings—there were other, juicier targets for them to lay into—Representative Blaine Luetkemeyer from Montana put into words what many were thinking:

"I understand that GameStop stock was short sold one hundred and forty percent...Mr. Plotkin, you made the comment in your testimony that you were not trying to manipulate stock...yet if you're short selling a stock one hundred and forty percent...on the outside looking in, it looks like that's exactly what you're doing...Explain to me why that's not manipulating a stock."

But it wasn't Gabe the congressman was taking aim at. It was the *system*.

"For us," Gabe answered. "I can't speak to other people that were short; any time we look to short a stock we locate a borrow, our systems actually force us to find a borrow, we always short stocks within the context of all the rules…"

From the short perspective, the manipulation was all on the other side of the trade. Gabe had shorted the stock because he believed it was going down, and others had piled into the trade because they agreed—to such an extent that shares were borrowed more than once. And clearly, the stock should have continued to go down. But it hadn't. Ultimately, the reason that it had instead gone up was murky. Could a bunch of unsophisticated, loosely coordinated retail traders actually launch such a short squeeze? Or was something deeper happening, which was yet to be uncovered?

If the committee was really looking to understand where Gabe's trade had gone wrong, they should have been focusing on the other side. The short trade was the one that had made sense.

It wasn't until three hours and forty minutes into the session that Representative Al Lawson, from Florida, finally asked Gabe about that other side. How, as the narrative went, an amateur investor could have caused the market to turn upside down and cost Gabe billions of dollars. How someone like Gabe, who had been a winner all his life, who knew that winning wasn't a sometime thing, but an all-time thing—could have been bested by a guy in his basement?

It was the question, no doubt, that Gabe had been asking himself every day since he'd closed his short position. Now, for the first time, he could try and answer it—because, for the first time in this entire ordeal, even though it was through that spiderweb of video screens, he was face-to-face with the mullet-headed, bandanna-wearing amateur who had nearly destroyed his fund.

"I think they saw an opportunity to drive the price of a stock higher," Gabe said, and as much as he tried to swallow it down, the pain was written in the deep lines above his eyes, "and today with social media and other means, there's the ability to collectively do so, that was a risk factor, you know, up until recently we'd never seen…they exploited an opportunity around short interest…"

But even as he spoke, the sparks began to light inside him. He was on the ground, wounded and bleeding—but he hadn't given up. From one sentence to the next, he seemed to push himself back up, first to his knees, then slowly, stronger, toward his feet.

"Us, and Melvin—we'll adapt, and I think the whole industry will have to adapt…"

When Congressman Lawson continued, asking what the industry needed to do to keep this from happening again, Gabe was already stepping forward, shaking the mud from his shoes. A fighter, getting up from the mat, strapping on the gloves again. Michael Jordan, walking onto the court the day after a rare loss, ready to start raining threes.

"I think to some degree markets are self-correcting. Moving forward, I don't think you're going to see stocks with the kind of short interest levels that we've seen prior to this year. I don't think investors like myself will want to be susceptible to these types of dynamics. I think there will be a lot closer monitoring of message boards…we have a data science team that will be looking at that…You know, whatever regulation that you guys come up with—certainly we'll abide by."

Even over livestream, the transformation was visible; in less than a minute, Gabe had gone from a bewildered victim to the professional athlete he'd always been. It was time to accept the loss and move on, because there were plenty more wins in his future.

As he had said, the market was self-correcting. The system would adapt. The stranger in the basement had bested Gabe, but now that he was revealed, now that the threat he represented was as sharp as the pixels on the screen in front of Gabe—he would not be able to beat Gabe again.

* * *

"Almost eight years ago, Baiju Bhatt and I founded Robinhood. We believed then, as we do now, that the financial system should be built to work for everyone, not just a select few."

Vlad Tenev, seated in perfect posture, in front of a low shelf supporting a couple of books that might have been biblical, and a trio of vases or vessels or urns that might have been ancient, was coasting on a cushion of air as he spoke TRUTH into the ether of the INTERNET.

"We dreamed of making investing more accessible, especially for people without a lot of money."

Vlad's words throbbed with the passion of a BELIEVER, and it didn't matter whether his sermon was reaching just the fifty-odd lawmakers who were gathered at the mount, or the millions upon millions who were watching in their homes.

"The stock market is a powerful wealth creator," he continued, "but almost half of US households—"

And when the first interruption came, from the chair herself, it seemed such a surprise that Vlad's stunned look was obvious to anyone who was watching.

"Mr. Tenev. I would like you to use your limited time to talk directly to what happened January 28, and your involvement in it."

And at first, maybe slightly more hesitant than he'd begun, Vlad tried to power through, quickly erecting the pillars of the Robinhood myth and message.

"We created Robinhood to economically empower all Americans by opening financial markets to them. I was born in Bulgaria, a country with a financial system that was on the verge of collapse. At the age of five, I immigrated with my family to America in search of a better life."

And again, he was gaining steam as he went from coasting on that cushion of air to dancing across a sparkling glade of water. He spoke, of course, of the democratization of finance. Of the educational resources of his platform. Of the wondrous fractional investments, the dividend reinvestments, and the recurring investments that his customers enjoyed; their steady diet of blue chip stocks and ETFs that had, in part, given that customer base a total value that "exceeds the net amount of money they have deposited by over 35 billion dollars."

"Our business model is working for everyday Americans," he added—but as high as he built those pillars, as hard as he tried to glide up to the elevated perch the mythology supported—within moments he found the interruption had only been the first salvo; by ten minutes into the hearing, the arrows were coming so fast and furious, they might as well have been a violent rain.

From Representative David Scott, of Georgia:

"Don't you see and agree that something very wrong happened here and that you're at the center of it?"

Representative Juan Vargas from California:

"Robin Hood is an English folk hero, thirteenth, fourteenth century, and he was supposed to steal...from the rich and give to the poor. Here, you almost have the opposite. You have the situation where you have the steal from the small retail investor and giving it to the large institutional investor."

And the many versions of a single question, parsed by Congressmen and -women from every angle: *Is payment for order flow even legal?*

Never mind that the people asking the questions were the very same lawmakers who crafted the rules and laws, who had helped build the system that had landed Vlad in their crosshairs. It was obvious he was not there as simply another witness to what had happened, like they'd mostly treated Gabe Plotkin—but to be a target. Accusations masquerading as questions, hurled at him in a mix of political grandstanding and real anger, all of them mined from the conspiracy-laden maelstrom that had been growing on social media since January 28.

Alexandria Ocasio-Cortez, the congresswoman from New York, summed up the attacks eight minutes after the five-hour mark:

"Mr. Tenev, Robinhood has engaged in a track record of outages, design failures and most recently what appears to be a failure to properly account for your own internal risk.

You've previously tried to blame clearinghouses for your need and scramble to raise 3.4 billion dollars in a matter of days... given Robinhood's track record, isn't it possible that the issue is not clearinghouses... but the fact that you simply didn't manage your own book?"

And from there, she'd pivoted to payment for order flow — highlighting that PFOF carried with it considerable chances for conflicts of interest, and furthermore, that the profits generated by the practice—though allowing Robinhood to provide commission-free trading—essentially meant "that trading on Robinhood isn't actually free to begin with?"

At first, though immediately on the defensive, Vlad answered the barrage of accusatory questions with as much poise and grace as he could muster. He spoke of how unusual—extraordinary—the events leading up to January 28 were; how the deposit requirement that had woken him from his sleep that morning had been ten times the requirement from just three days earlier; how seriously they had taken the act of restricting buying of GME, but how infinitely worse it would have been had they prevented customers from selling, making them unable to access money when perhaps they needed it.

But by the end of the session, his posture was suffering; his jacket and tie disheveled, and his cheeks flushed.

When he finally responded to Ocasio-Cortez's unyielding attack—"Certainly, Congresswoman, Robinhood is a for-profit business"—he was clearly flustered. And in another part of the hearing, when things turned, inevitably, to whether Robinhood had "gamified" the stock market with its amateur-friendly app, there was little he could do but throw up his hands.

"Look, I'm sorry for what happened," he apologized, no longer coasting on air, but gasping for it. "I apologize. I'm not gonna say that Robinhood did everything perfect…"

But this, in his words, was a 1 in 3.5 million occurrence event. "One that had never been seen before in capital markets."

He didn't believe it had anything to do with gamification. A word which the congressmen and -women tossed at him like it was evil incarnate—ironic, considering the entire episode revolved around a mob of retail traders trying to prop up the stock of a company that existed only because of the American public's love of games.

Although Vlad wouldn't have said it himself, if anyone had gamified Wall Street, it was the American people. The very populace that had put these congressmen and -women into office. They were the ones buying GameStop for the expressed reason to take down Wall Street.

In the end, it all boiled down to a single question— could this happen again? Vlad was certain that with their new financial cushion, even if it did, his company could handle it. But even so, he might have felt that he wasn't the right person to ask—because as slick and as cool and as addictive as his app might be, he was only the middleman.

Sure, when you were the middleman, when things went wrong, you were inevitably in the *middle*; but if Wall Street *had* been gamified, if the stock market *had* turned into some vast video game, Robinhood was just the console.

The hedge funds—Melvin, Gabe Plotkin—and the retail traders—the bandanna in the basement—were the players. If a video game was broken, if its software seemed suddenly filled with bugs—you didn't blame the console, and you didn't blame the players.

You either blamed the people who built the game, or you blamed whoever was powerful enough to change its code once it had already been set in motion.

*   *   *

"I want to be perfectly clear. We had no role in Robinhood's decision to limit trading in GameStop…I first learned of Robinhood's trading restrictions only after they were publicly announced…"

Ken Griffin spoke calmly, carefully, and precisely into the camera, rarely blinking, as if even the act of blinking was something he did by choice and not out of necessity. He appeared confident, if not comfortable, facing the powerful House Committee, and his tone was that of a man who had many important things to do that day; he was there because it was unavoidable, and he would answer any questions the congressmen and -women asked—but he didn't intend to repeat himself.

"During the period of frenzied retail equities trading, Citadel Securities was able to provide continuous liquidity every minute of every trading day. When others were unable or unwilling to handle the heavy volumes, Citadel Securities was there. On Wednesday, January twenty-seventh, we executed 7.4 billion shares on behalf of retail investors. To put this into perspective, on that day Citadel Securities executed more shares for retail investors than the entire average daily volume of the entire US equities market in 2019."

The visual background behind him couldn't have appeared more institutional; off-white, with perfectly symmetric panels on the wall, above a matching, similarly off-white set of cabinets. Ken's suit was framed on either side by equidistant potted plants, leaves crawling down the sides like frightened vines. If potted plants could talk, these looked like they might scream or, at the very least, whimper. The entire visual effect was somewhere between a broadcast from the break room in a chiropractor's office and an infomercial shoot pawning some shady diabetes medicine.

And as the hearing progressed from the opening statements into the inquisition, it was obvious that Ken's patience would be taxed, perhaps beyond its usual limits. Although some of the questions were well meaning, many seemed—unintentionally—designed to show how little the gathered congressional committee actually *understood* what it was that Citadel *did*, or how the financial system actually *worked*, or why dragging Ken in front of them was a waste of everyone's *time*. He was clearly playing a game they barely comprehended, in a field well above their areas of expertise.

As Ken tried—as patiently as a man who definitely had not built a throne out of the bones of his competitors—to explain things like T+2 processing, competitive market maker spreads, and how Citadel Securities saved customers billions via best execution models, he could imagine most of his questioners shriveling away, like the plants behind him. The simple truth was, the technology had moved so fast, the financial system had grown so complex, that if you hadn't been on the inside, every day, for decades, you had very little chance of really grasping what a man like Ken did to keep the economy pumping along. It was akin to a time-traveling anthropologist from a highly complex civilization coming into contact with some ancient community—but it was the ancient community that was trying to decipher and translate the anthropologist's complex language, not the other way around. They simply wouldn't—and didn't—have the experience or the tools to understand.

Which was probably why most of the ire and attacks were aimed at Vlad and Robinhood, and only a handful of the congressmen and -women felt brave enough to come at Ken. Vlad was an easy target, not just because he looked so accessible and inviting, like the kind of friendly, wide-eyed guy you might find volunteering to work the dunking booth at a traveling carnival; but what Robinhood did—and had done—was so damn easy to understand. They put themselves out there in such simple terms—hell, that was their business model, to simplify, make accessible, level, and yes, gamify, things that were *supposed* to be prohibitively complex.

So it was no surprise that when one of the congressional inquisitors—Representative Juan Vargas, of California—finally did turn toward Ken, the congressman was jumping off from the simple narrative surrounding Robinhood and its seeming betrayal of its user base:

"Did anyone in your organization since January first contact Robinhood?"

But from Ken's reaction, it appeared to be the sort of foolish question he might have boiled an underling for asking:

"Are you asking if we've had *contact* with Robinhood?" And then he clarified, as if it needed clarification. "We of course are talking to Robinhood routinely in the ordinary course of business. We manage a substantial proportion of their order flow."

And when the congressman tried to tunnel down further, to an actual accusation:

"Did you talk to them about restricting or doing anything to prevent people from buying GameStop?"

Ken's response came back tinged with a vigor anyone who had ever met him—and walked away with all four limbs still attached—would have recognized:

"Let me be perfectly clear. ABSOLUTELY NOT."

Ken was so adamant in his answer that he refrained from blinking for the next full beat, his visage so still that one might have wondered if his wireless had gone down.

And for the most part, there was very little that was asked of him beyond that, that truly related to the events surrounding GameStop. When Representative Rashida Tlaib took her turn at Ken from the virtual podium, she didn't mention GameStop at all:

"As we all know, the wealthiest ten percent own eighty-four percent of all stocks. In fact, fifty percent of American families own no stock at all. I say this to emphasize that to many of my residents, the stock market is simply a casino for the rich…and when you all screw up…the people end up paying the tab."

From there, she segued right into a question about "high frequency trading," the computerized strategy of trading ahead of the market—but what she was asking about was so complex, it was impossible for Ken to even begin to answer in a way that might satisfy her.

If anything, though she was making an important point

about a tangentially related financial practice, the moment encapsulated how absurd it was for someone like Ken to even be called to a hearing like this. If Ken was on trial—which he clearly wasn't—he would have expected to be judged by a jury of his peers. But Ken Griffin, and Citadel, *had* no peers.

During Representative Vargas's questioning, the congressman had scored what appeared to be a significant point when, before pressing Ken on his contact with Robinhood, he'd asked:

"Mr. Griffin. How many people are in the room with you?" And Ken had answered—"There are five people, including myself."

But the point the representative had thought he'd made—that Wall Street CEOs like Ken had teams of suits around them, protecting them, advising them, shielding them from foolish wastes of time like, say, pointless hearings—was only part of the equation. Ken had a team around him because what he did was so complex and complicated, it was almost impossible to separate him from the system surrounding him.

By the end of the five-and-a-half-hour hearing, there was little doubt that the gathered congressmen and -women were no closer to understanding what had really happened that week in January than they had been the day before. There was also no doubt that Ken was at the center of what had happened—because Ken, and Citadel, were at the center of just about everything that happened in the US financial markets. But the questions asked of him illuminated very little, because either they weren't the right questions, or there *were* no right questions.

Whether Citadel had actively pressured Robinhood to restrict the buying of GameStop was an easy query for Ken to answer—because *of course* they hadn't. Why would they need to? Robinhood's clearing deposit requirements had made it impossible for Vlad's company to do anything else.

Did payment for order flow necessitate conflicts of interest, by turning Robinhood's users into their product? Theoretically, sure, but whose fault was that, really? Citadel, who made money by providing Robinhood with the most efficient, cheapest trades? Robinhood, who also made money, but could thus give their customers the ability to trade for free? Or the users themselves, who could also make money, without ever paying a penny in commissions?

Was "high frequency trading" or "trading ahead of the market" something sketchy and dangerous and corruptible? Christ, almost certainly yes, but who the hell really understood what any of that meant anyway? The odds were, if you truly did understand it, you were probably doing it, not trying to come up with coherent questions to ask people like Ken.

Maybe it would have been better to have kept things simple. Though a few of the representatives had danced around the subject, they could have asked Ken the only question that truly applied:

Why, exactly, had he invested $2 billion in Melvin Capital—a hedge fund that had just lost half of its value in a matter of days? Even if you didn't call it a bailout, why would a man like Ken Griffin invest in a hemorrhaging hedge fund, no matter how much of a star Gabe Plotkin might be?

Could Ken's rivalry with Steve Cohen have really been enough of an impetus to make Ken want to get into a fund, in presumably favorable fashion—even though that fund had just exploded in such a public, and perhaps existential way?

Or was Ken propping up Melvin for some other reason? Was there something deeper going on?

The conspiracy theorists were almost definitely wrong: as Ken had testified, he hadn't pressured Robinhood to restrict the buying of GameStop to save Melvin and the other short-selling hedge funds—and obviously, he hadn't needed to. Robinhood's clearance requirements made sure of that.

But, one might have asked, wouldn't Ken and Citadel have been fully aware of what those clearance requirements were going to be, and how Robinhood would have needed to react? Wouldn't Citadel have known—Thursday morning, January 28—that Robinhood wouldn't be able to meet their deposit requirements without monkeying with the buy side of GameStop?

If a firm like Citadel really was able to make money by trading ahead of the market—wasn't this a situation where a firm like Citadel would know what was about to happen, ahead of the market? Wouldn't they have been able to use that knowledge, if they were so inclined, in numerous ways?

Perhaps, if the right questions had been asked—or even if there were any right questions—Ken's presence at the hearing might have made sense. Ground, if not clarity, might have been gained, toward understanding the tendrils connecting GameStop, Melvin, Robinhood, and the system as a whole.

But as it was, Ken's rarely blinking attendance seemed to have offered as much clarity as the two potted plants behind him. The truth was, from all appearances, the House Committee hadn't summoned Ken to answer questions about GameStop. They'd summoned him to prove to themselves that they still *could.*

And he'd given them five-and-a-half hours of his time. Which was more, he might have felt, than this absurd moment in history deserved.

Ken wasn't some kid with a cat poster and a Magic 8-Ball sitting in some basement in some suburb of Boston, after all. He was the CEO of Citadel.

And he had an economy to run.

CHAPTER TWENTY-EIGHT

And once again the camera flicked on.

"Thank you, Chairwoman Waters...I am happy to discuss with the committee my purchases of GameStop shares and my discussions of their fair value on social media. It is true that my investment in that company multiplied in value many times. For that I feel enormously fortunate. I also believe the current price of the shares demonstrates that I have been right about the company..."

The moment was somehow surreal and routine at the same time; Keith Gill at his desk in his basement, talking into his bright red streaming microphone while he sat in his *Game of Thrones* faux leather chair. The whiteboard was behind him, but now sporting nothing but his favorite cat poster—the kitten hanging from a paw, over the slogan "Hang in there!"

"A few things I am not. I am not a cat. I am not an institutional investor. Nor am I a hedge fund..."

But today, the red bandanna was not tied around Keith's

head; it was hanging from a corner of the poster, fully visible to the camera—perhaps a nod to how significant he knew the event was. Another nod—his colorful T-shirts, so often sporting more cats or video game slogans, had been replaced by a stiffly ironed jacket and tightly tied tie. True, the jacket looked like it had just come out of the cleaner's bag and the tie was so shiny, if you flipped it over, you might expect to find the price tag still attached. But there was no doubt, Keith was taking this seriously, and though he didn't look as much like an awkward deer caught in the headlights as his counterpart, Gabe Plotkin, it was clear, as the old children's show used to say, "One of these things is not like the other."

"I'm just an individual whose investment in GameStop and posts on social media were based upon my own research and analysis…"

The sense that he didn't really belong in the lineup of highly sophisticated professionals that had been called to the congressional hearing had been building since the list of witnesses had been made public. Vlad Tenev, chief executive officer, Robinhood Markets, Inc.; Kenneth C. Griffin, chief executive officer, Citadel LLC; Gabriel Plotkin, chief executive officer, Melvin Capital Management LP; Steve Huffman, chief executive officer, cofounder, Reddit.

Keith Gill.

No job title, no impressive description, not even a friendly Brockton, Massachusetts. Just some dude named Keith Gill.

"Two important factors, based entirely on publicly available information, gave me confidence that GameStop was undervalued. First, the market was underestimating the prospects of GameStop's legacy business and overestimating the likelihood of bankruptcy. I grew up playing video games and shopping at GameStop, and I plan to continue shopping there…"

A dude, who was still, despite the massive drop in the share price of GME since Robinhood had punched a hole in the short squeeze, worth close to $20 million, at least "on paper."

"Second, I believe that GameStop has the potential to reinvent itself as the ultimate destination for gamers within the rapidly growing 200 billion dollar gaming industry…"

Although Keith had temporarily paused his YOLO updates to deal with the growing fallout from what he'd—arguably—started, and he'd likewise taken time off YouTube to be with his family and shield himself from a level of attention that even someone who had once aspired to a career in professional sports could not have imagined, his thesis hadn't changed—nor had his belief in GameStop dimmed. If it hadn't been for the media attention, he would very likely have been right where he was—professing his love for GME to the camera, with or without a congressional audience.

"When I wrote and spoke about GameStop on social media with other individual investors our conversations were no different from people in a bar, or on a golf course, or at home, talking or arguing about a stock…"

Because he still believed, and would always believe, that professing your love for a company like GameStop was as right, fair, legal—and really, as American—as the stock market itself.

As he put it in his own words, as he neared the end of his opening statement to the House Committee, to the millions who might be watching the livestream, and to the faces of the other players in the drama that had unfolded—Gabe Plotkin, Vlad Tenev, Ken Griffin—whom he was "meeting" for the first time—the fact that he had been communicating via "social media platforms" rather than standing at the head of a boardroom in a Wall Street office or over Zoom to a team of analysts or portfolio managers didn't make any difference.

"The idea that I used social media to promote GameStop stock to unwitting investors and influence the market is preposterous."

As if Keith Gill, one-time-near-four-minute-miler, son of a truck driver and an RN, a guy who'd spent most of his adult life unemployed or barely employed, could have tricked anyone into buying GME.

"My posts did not cause the movement of billions of dollars into GameStop shares."

As if Keith Gill could have personally caused a revolution that had nearly taken down one of the biggest hedge funds on Wall Street.

It was a ridiculous, insane notion. A revolution like that came from somewhere much deeper than some gathering of "apes" and "retards" on some subreddit in the basement of the Internet. A revolution like that came from something much deeper, even, than the deep, deep, deep fucking research of some dude in his basement, some kid from Brockton.

And when Keith had finally finished his testimony— when he'd finally made it through the five-and-a-half hours of the hearing, barely answering a handful of questions during the event because really, who was he anyway?—

he turned off his camera, glanced at the comments flashing one after another down the WallStreetBets board—and then shifted back to his trading account.

As he looked at that beautiful ticker, GME, multiplied 50,000 times, once for each share he still held—he knew what he needed to do next.

Buy *moar.*

Because, well, even after everything.

He just really liked the stock.

CHAPTER TWENTY-NINE

Five Hundred Forty Madison Avenue, thirty-second floor. A stone's throw from Gabe Plotkin's Melvin Capital, five buildings over and ten floors up.

A similar glass-and-steel office, also empty and quiet and dark. Another ghost ship floating in the sea of vacant skyscrapers, picture windows like portholes looking out over a vista that mostly remained cold and dead. Another near-lifeless hub, the heart of a cadaver that, like Melvin, somehow still had that functioning circulatory system, veins and capillaries reaching out like spokes to temporary offices and second homes all over the world.

Richard Mashaal, CEO of Senvest Management, in one of those temporary offices, in one of those second homes, leaned back from his computer, and let the tension finally drain from his face, neck, and shoulders. Usually his appearance was well coiffed and precise; but at the moment, he was disheveled. His hair was a mess and one of the buttons of his shirt had worked itself free. His left sleeve was rolled up too far, and his suit jacket had fallen off the back of his chair to the floor—but he didn't give a damn. He looked like he'd just been through a war, which made sense, because what he'd just experienced was as near a financial equivalent to pitched combat as one could get. A profound, career-changing experience; but unlike his counterpart centered five buildings over, Richard hadn't lost the fight. Quite the opposite, his victory was so extreme, it would go down in the annals of Wall Street as one of the best trades anyone had ever made.

Unlike many of his Wall Street counterparts, Richard wasn't a financial celebrity. "Mashaal" was far from a household name, and even in the rarified world of hedge funds, he wasn't particularly well known. Part of this anonymity was by choice; Richard and his co-CIO Brian Gonick had made little effort to mingle with the hedge fund set, even as their own shop had grown from a tiny $5 million seed in the early nineties, primarily from friends and family, to a still relatively small but totally respectable $2 billion pre-pandemic valuation.

Given their firm's unique investment profile, their stand-offishness was little surprise. The contrarian approach to public equities wasn't for everyone; seeking out and investing in unappreciated, dismissed, misunderstood, and yes, unloved stocks was inherently risky. Putting money into companies that most other funds were avoiding, or betting against, was a volatile strategy that yielded a balance sheet that never ran in a straight line. There were down quarters, down years—but when Richard and his team picked correctly, the gains could be impressive. As a contrarian investor, you didn't need to be right often, because when you were, it was—explosive.

Richard's tendency to swim against the current probably

had to do with his background; he'd grown up in Montreal, not New York. His father was an entrepreneur, who'd made part of his fortune by bringing to Canada the miniature, ubiquitous, anti-shoplifting tags found attached to the sleeves and linings of clothes in most retail stores around the world. After Wharton and the University of Chicago, Richard had returned to Canada to focus on the public equity arm of the family business, which then morphed into his fund—Senvest Management, named after his father's "sensormatic security tags"—with its headquarters firmly planted in New York, the financial capital of the world.

Though over the next decade, some of Senvest's most notable wins might have been on the short side—in particular, a short position on Insys Therapeutics, a biomedical company that allegedly had pushed a synthetic form of fentanyl through shady, kickback-driven relationships with corrupt physicians—Richard and Brian had always been more interested in identifying diamonds in the rough; companies that the rest of Wall Street had turned their backs on, but still had the potential for transformation. And when Senvest went long, they didn't tend to sit on the sidelines, watch the stock-ticker, and pray; they liked to get involved. When they bought shares, they considered themselves part owners of the company, and they regularly engaged with management, trying to push them in the direction that would be beneficial for everyone.

When Richard, Brian, and the Senvest team had stumbled onto GameStop in early September of last year, the stock had been trading in the $6–$7 range, and for what seemed like good reason. The world was rapidly going digital, while GameStop was mired in the physical: stores, game cartridges and disks, plastic consoles. Management, too, appeared to be anachronistically myopic, unable to take advantage of the natural advantages the company might have in the rapidly booming gaming space. It was no wonder the stock had such a huge short volume—anyone who'd ever cracked a business textbook could smell the "melting ice cube" from a thousand miles away.

But Richard and Brian saw something else, too. Similar to what Michael Burry had observed, Microsoft and Play-Station were about to launch new versions of their gaming devices—physical consoles, which had to be bought some-where, not downloaded through the magic of the Internet. And second—and perhaps more important—there was Ryan Cohen, the e-commerce genius, who had bested Amazon in the multibillion-dollar online pet supply domain, throwing his money into the stock, and further, throwing himself into the fray with his angry letter to the GameStop board.

To the Senvest team, these seemed like two positive indicators in that ocean of red that transformation wasn't the wild bet it might seem. Added to that, the crazy short volume—at the time, already touching 100 percent of the float. This, in itself, was attractive; all those short sellers needed to borrow the shares they wanted to sell from some-one, and a fund like Senvest could make a pretty steady return lending out those shares.

So the decision was made—and Richard's team began to buy. Quietly, at first, because the last thing a fund wanted anyone to know was that they were buying shares in what they saw as an undervalued stock. Little by little, they picked up shares, starting with a small enough position that it wouldn't impact the market. A 2 percent position, which became 3 percent—and the more confident Richard and Brian became that they were onto something real, the deeper they stuck their feet into the churning water.

When they hit 5 percent of the stock, they were required to file their position with the SEC—notifying the public what they were up to—but still, somehow, their interest remained mostly under the radar, perhaps because, by then, the business media had become distracted by the drama unfolding between the WallStreetBets mob and Melvin. A little Montreal-born fund named after an anti-shoplifting tag couldn't possibly compete with such a movie-ready, David versus Goliath narrative.

By the time the stock began really popping, Senvest had acquired around 7 percent of the available shares. It wasn't quite the investment that Ryan Cohen had put into the company, but it was enough to suddenly have a voice with management—and as was their fashion, Richard and his team immediately went to work trying to push the company toward the transformation they believed was possible. Through the end of 2020 and into the beginning of January, they did their best to convince the GameStop board to stop battling with Cohen and bring him inside. Although Senvest had already doubled, then tripled their investment—they knew that with Cohen helping to call the shots, GameStop might truly have a shot at becoming an e-commerce giant, rather than an aging brick-and-mortar dinosaur.

When the news hit, on January 11, that management had heeded their suggestions, and Cohen was officially joining the board of the company—Richard had known that the fuse had officially been lit. As the stock began to fly—into the $30s by January 13, the $40s a day later, it was clear

Senvest was sitting on a huge win. The question became, how long could they ride that wave?

It was perhaps the most difficult part of investing—knowing when to accept that you'd won. From Richard's position on the other side of the trade, he could only guess at what Gabe Plotkin and Melvin's thinking was, as they watched the stock rising. They'd originally shorted the company at around $40 a share, and had rode their own winning wave all the way down to $5. They could have walked away with a fortune—and instead, inscrutably, they'd ridden it all the way back up to $40 and beyond, and still, apparently, had been doubling down.

Richard did not intend to make the same mistake. The short squeeze in full effect by the beginning of the week of January 25, he prepared his trading team to accept their win.

Picking the moment to exit a stock was as much an art as it was a science. But in this particular case, at the height of this particular war—that moment hit Richard like it had been fired from an enemy ship's cannon.

Elon Musk's tweet—Gamestonk!!—at 4:08 on the afternoon of January 26, which sent the stock spiraling higher, destroying whatever short positions were still standing and triggering the chaos that would ensue soon after, via Robinhood, Citadel, and whoever else the conspiracy theory of the day decided to implicate—was as clear a signal as Richard could have ever asked for.

Peak momentum, he told his traders, and right there, they began the process of unloading the bulk of their shares.

Beginning in the premarket the next morning, the stock was all over the map. But Richard's team, spread out at desks in cities all over the country, sold into the frenzy at a dizzying pace, Richard and Brian orchestrating via e-mail and text and Zoom.

And by that afternoon, it was done. Senvest had sold all their shares, at a profit of upwards of $700 million. All of it, on a single trade.

In normal times, under normal circumstances, they would have spent the rest of the day celebrating. Champagne corks flying, music blaring, dancing on desks, maybe a kicked-over Bloomberg terminal or two.

Instead, Richard Mashaal sat alone, at his desk. Later, he'd go for a long bike ride on the beach, perhaps start planning a company trip to Park City for skiing, the first time most of them would see each other since the pandemic had overtaken their lives.

And as he sat there, his mind was already thinking ahead, to what his company's next move might be. When everything had been going crazy, before they'd exited their position, one of Richard's younger traders had once pointed out to him that, on the Reddit boards, the amateur traders liked to call profits "tendies."

Seven hundred million was probably the whole damn chicken; even so, the funny thing was, when something tasted that good, even when you ate a lot of it—it didn't make you feel full.

It just made you hungry for more.

AFTER

On February 19, one day after the congressional hearing on the short squeeze that rocked the world, Keith Gill posted his first YOLO update on WallStreetBets in over two weeks. According to the screenshot attached to the post, Keith had added an exclamation point to his testimony—putting more of his money behind his unwavering belief that GameStop was at the beginning of its journey into the digital age and not nearing the end. Despite the fact that the price of GME had plummeted from its highs of near $500 a share after Robinhood's actions had arguably put a lid on the WSB-powered short squeeze to the low $40s, Keith had announced, through his post, that he was as bullish as ever, doubling his stake to 100,000 shares of the stock, in addition to $1.5 million in call options.

If the price action of GME in the weeks and months that followed Keith's post told us anything, it's that Keith was not alone in his love for the stock; though the price remained stable in the $40s for the next few days, by the end of the week, GME was skyrocketing again. The impetus for the sudden climb—from a close of around $45 a share on Wednesday, February 23, to a staggering high-of-day $142.90 on February 26, is still unclear, though it probably had a number of causes: Keith's continued support rallying the WSB faithful—which by that time was closing in on a dizzying 10 million subscribers. The resignation of GameStop's CFO, Jim Bell, which may have represented a shift in forward strategy, to more align with the digital dreams for the company of Ryan Cohen and his supporters. And a cryptic tweet by Cohen himself, which landed on Twitter at 1:57 p.m. on the twenty-fourth, consisting of a photo of a McDonald's ice cream cone along with a frog emoji. Though Cohen didn't include an explanation along with the photo, many assumed he was telling the world that he intended to fix GameStop, the way McDonald's had set out to fix its famously unreliable ice cream machines.

Whatever the initial reason, the GME roller coaster was back on its tracks; over the next twelve weeks, the stock price swung as high as $283 and continued its volatile seesawing as more news continued to feed the narrative that GameStop had finally seen the light and was going to try to change its fundamentals to coincide more clearly with its suddenly skyrocketing valuation. To that end, the company sold 3.5 million shares of its stock, raising over $500 million, to lower its debt and invest in an online-focused future. GameStop's CEO, George Sherman, announced that he was stepping down—to a reported payout of $179 million, a happy accident of the rocketing stock price rather than being performance-related in a traditional sense—while Ryan Cohen was named chairman, signifying management's intent to use the moment to its advantage, as they took direct aim at turning GameStop into the e-commerce gargantuan Keith Gill had always believed it could be.

At the moment of this writing, the stock still sits at a healthy $159.48, putting the company's valuation at well over $11 billion. It remains to be seen whether this valuation is somehow reasonable—if Keith Gill is right, if GameStop can make good on its new mission to become the Amazon of video games, rather than a brick-and-mortar throwback like Blockbuster—or if the short sellers had been prescient all along, and the smoke and mirrors of this shared, Reddit-inspired delusion will eventually dissipate, and the stock will plummet back to Earth.

But the bigger question might be: Does it really matter what GameStop management does? Will the company's fundamentals—*any* company's fundamentals—have any bearing on its stock price in the world we are moving toward, where a group of amateurs on social media can move markets?

Where a well-constructed tweet, or a particularly humorous meme, or an inspiring YOLO post can shift billions of dollars into a company's valuation?

In such a post-GameStop-revolutionary future, is there really such a thing as a melting ice cube anymore? Or is every stock now—maybe the market itself—more like an untethered balloon?

When you stick a pin in a balloon, it doesn't plummet toward the ground. It fires off at odd angles, sometimes shooting up to extreme heights, spinning and spiraling and seesawing—until it eventually runs out of air. Then it might drift back to the ground; or it might defy ration and reason, get caught in a stiff breeze—and rise up, and up, forever.

ACKNOWLEDGMENTS

First and foremost, I need to thank my kids, Asher and Arya, for dragging me into every GameStop we've ever walked by or driven past; when this story first exploded into the news and I started getting calls from everyone I knew telling me that this was something I was born to write, I was already primed and ready. Enormous thanks also to my brilliant agents, Eric Simonoff and Matt Snyder, who made two of those calls, pushing me to dive down this crazy rabbit hole. I am also indebted to my fantastic editor, Wes Miller, for working round the clock during this strangest of years to help make this one of the best writing experiences of my career; and to Andy Dodds, for helping to put together a book tour in such an unusual time. Thanks also to my incredible team in Hollywood for their faith, encouragement, and creativity—Mike Deluca, who has been riding with me since Vegas, Pam Abdy, and Katie Martin Kelley—and megaproducer Aaron Ryder, whose movies have been thrilling me for years. Also enormous thanks to our screenwriters, Lauren Schuker Blum and Rebecca Angelo; I can't wait to see what you do with this.

ACKNOWLEDGMENTS

A project like this lives and dies by its sources. I was fortunate to have had the help and insight of many, most of whom need to remain anonymous. A special thanks to Ross Gerber, who taught me a lot about Tesla and finance. Thanks also to Ben Wehrman, one of my Twitter gurus—and to Twitter itself, which, along with Reddit and the resources they both provided, made this book even possible.

Most important, and as always, thank you Tonya, my secret weapon. And Asher, Arya, Bugsy, Bagel, and my parents—you make it all worthwhile.

ABOUT THE AUTHOR

Ben Mezrich is the *New York Times* bestselling author of *The Accidental Billionaires* (adapted by Aaron Sorkin into the David Fincher film *The Social Network*) and *Bringing Down the House* (adapted into the No. 1 box office hit film *21*), as well as many other bestselling books. His books have sold over six million copies worldwide. Mezrich's forthcoming novel, *The Midnight Ride*, will be published by GCP in early 2022.